THE

Faith

— OF —

St. Nick

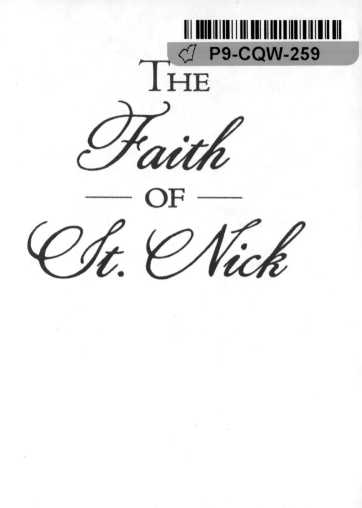

Published by Barbour Publishing, Inc., P.O. Box 719, Uhrichsville, Ohio
44683, www.barbourbooks.com

*Our mission is to publish and distribute inspirational products offering
exceptional value and biblical encouragement to the masses.*

ecpa Member of the
Evangelical Christian
Publishers Association

Printed in the United States of America.

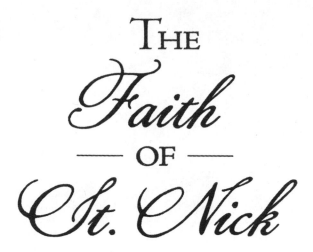

THE Faith — OF — St. Nick

AN ADVENT DEVOTIONAL

ANN NICHOLS

BARBOUR
PUBLISHING

For Saint Nicholas
and his ministry that has reached
down through the centuries.

With much love and many thanks to
George, Sara, Jay, and Kasia who have
patiently traveled this journey with me
to meet the real Saint Nicholas!

And with love to my parents, Sara and Sayre,
who from my earliest childhood
gave me a great love of the Advent season
and of Christmas!

The faith of Saint Nick and the Advent season. . .

If ever the life of a Christian reflected the Lord's, it was the man we refer to as Saint Nick!

It was his faith in Jesus Christ that enabled him to do the many deeds of mercy, charitable acts, and wonders that we, nearly 1700 years after he lived, are still familiar with.

It is my pleasure, during these thoughtful and joyful days leading up to the glorious commemoration of the birth of Christ, to visit the life of this celebrated man of faith. In the spirit of an Advent calendar we will "open a window" through fictionalized scenes based on real events in the life of Saint Nicholas each day leading up to and including Christmas Day.

The gift of Jesus' birth was not wasted on Saint Nicholas. He gratefully and faithfully took that gift—the gift of salvation whose mystery was unfolded in a very big way at Christ's birth—built his life upon it and shared the Lord's Gospel with all.

I first started studying about Saint Nicholas to answer my young children's questions about his alter ego, Santa Claus. I was surprised when my study into the real Saint Nicholas's life brought me to new levels of Christian understanding and faith. My children are grown now, but I am still studying and still learning from Saint Nick and the dynamic time in Christian history in which he lived.

His life proves how just one man, with faith in the Lord Jesus Christ, really can make a difference in the world.

Happy Advent from Saint Nicholas. . .and me!

Ann Nichols

EXPECTATION AND ANTICIPATION

And so it was, that, while they were there,
the days were accomplished that she should be
delivered. And she brought forth her firstborn son.
LUKE 2:6–7 KJV

"And I will put enmity between you and the woman,
and between your offspring and hers; he will crush
your head, and you will strike his heel."
GENESIS 3:15 NIV

*I*t's December first!

Are there any dates on the calendar that make a Christian happier than this day? Christmas feelings swoop in to fill our souls! Christmas is ahead of us! Even the cold of winter outside adds to the cozy feelings of love and warmth, peace and hope, faith and music, giving and family that rush in to greet us. Something about this day makes us believe that the world will be all right.

There is a reason for this expectation. The season it heralds—Christmastime—is exactly what makes it so that the world will be perfect again. Without Christ's First Advent as a baby, His Second Advent, as reigning Lord, would never be.

Expectations run high this time of year. Whether it's the anticipation of a perfect holiday gathering, amazing decorations, or best-ever family time, we place a lot of importance on everything being just so. And even though our plans sometimes lead to disappointments, thankfully our God always remains the same. Jesus' Second Advent will come just as surely as His first.

In a roundabout way, this brings us to the beginning of the life of Saint Nicholas. Most don't know it but Saint Nick almost didn't make it into existence. When he was born into the Greco/Roman world around AD 250, it was a very tough time for Christians. In fact, it's very likely that Saint Nicholas's parents had been in prison for proclaiming Christ in the months just before Nicholas made his appearance along the timeline of men.

Let's open our first window into his life and see the day he was born!

The cry of a newborn child in the seaport city of Patara burst through the door.

"She did it!" The dignified merchant Theophany turned and exclaimed to his brother.

"Praise God! It's a miracle." His brother, the leader of the church in Patara, agreed.

Theophany's happiness however quickly turned to dismay. He could hear the beautiful sounds of his child crying but nothing from his dear wife. "But is Joanna okay?" She had become so sick during the persecution.

"Have faith," Theophany's brother encouraged.

As the sound of the child continued to grow through the door, Theophany's faith swelled. The child he had been eagerly anticipating had finally been born! He would not let doubt enter his mind at this moment. Joanna might not be strong physically, but there were few who matched her in faith and will.

The door opened.

Theophany's gaze immediately went to his wife.

She was smiling at him!

"You're okay?" he asked softly as he went to her side. He had to make sure Joanna was well before he turned to the child.

"The pain is gone," she said, and he could tell that she was amazed to report that. "Totally gone. With the birth of our son, I am quite well."

"Son?" he questioned softly. Relief and joy

filled his voice, which was renowned for being so strong that it easily carried over the noisy quay to the captains of his ships but was now barely more than a whisper.

Joanna looked toward their child as he squirmed and fussed beside her. He was swaddled tightly in the fine, soft fabric she had woven for him. She motioned for Theophany to lift him. "My love, may I present you with your son."

Theophany reached for the precious bundle and for the first time looked into the eyes of his child, the baby who would grow to be one of the greatest men of faith ever to live.

"Our son," he said and smiled at Joanna before retuning his gaze to the baby. "Praise God!"

Baby Nicholas stopped crying and looked calmly and deeply into the eyes of the man who would teach him the most important thing in the world—about baby Jesus who had been born in Bethlehem just a little over 250 years earlier.

Holding his son close to his heart, Theophany leaned down and kissed his wife. "Thank you, my love. My feelings for this child—they are much more than even what I expected."

Expectations are a funny thing.

Sometimes our expectations are so high that there's no way they can be met, but sometimes we have hopes that are far exceeded by anything we can imagine.

Thankfully, it's rare for a parent to be disappointed with their newborn, and normally the feelings of love toward this new human are, as Theophany says above, much more than what parents expect.

That's how it is for Christians and our relationship to the Christ child, too.

The "Christmas feelings" of love and goodwill won't disappoint as long as our focus is on the Child who came that historic day a little over 2,000 years ago. All the cozy trimmings of Christmas—and the time leading up to it—are wonderful, but not necessary to the glorious celebration.

All we need for that is Christ.

He really does fulfill all our expectations—if we but let Him!

Prepare Your Heart for Christmas

Share with your family or friends something you are eagerly anticipating during this Advent season. On Christmas Day see if that expectation was met.

Often it's those closest to us who help God fulfill our expectations.

Jesus, as I await with anticipation this year's celebration of Your First Advent, let me never forget that there will just as surely be Your Second Advent. Come, Lord Jesus, come! Amen.

Prayer

*"But who can endure the day of His coming? And who
can stand when He appears? . . . I will be a swift witness
against sorcerers, against adulterers, against perjurers,
against those who exploit wage earners and widows and
orphans, and against those who turn away an alien—
Because they do not fear Me," says the LORD of hosts.*

MALACHI 3:2, 5 NKJV

*"But rise and stand on your feet; for I have appeared
to you for this purpose, to make you a minister and
a witness both of the things which you have seen
and of the things which I will yet reveal to you."*

ACTS 26:16 NKJV

On this second day of Advent, let's pause to
remember the importance of prayer during this holy
time of year. As the activities of the season unfold, we
must pray for our loved ones, for the world, for the
Church, and for those who will be traveling to arrive
home in time for Christmas in twenty-three days!

This is something Saint Nicholas's parents did even before their child was born. Symeon Metaphrastes, a secretary of state of the Roman Empire of the East, wrote in his tenth century *Life of Saint Nicholas*, "The infant was sanctified by the prayer and piety of both his parents, so that from his youth Nicholas's heart and soul were devoted to God."

The power of praying parents!

But not even Theophany and Joanna could have imagined how their prayers for their child would immediately be shown.

Let's open this second window into Nicholas's life and see what happened!

❋

Theophany, Joanna, and everyone at their home, where the Church in Patara met, hardly wanted to voice what they had just witnessed.

Nicholas's uncle had just baptized the babe when Nicholas—still just a newborn—stood on his own.

"How can this be?" Joanna asked afterward as she held their now sleeping child close.

"God's ways are not our own, Joanna," Theophany answered. "Perhaps He is giving us a sign as to the life our Nicholas is to lead."

"But he is just a baby!" The truth was, for all that she was a woman of great faith, the incident had scared Joanna. To those given great gifts, great things were asked. She had

no problem with being a martyr herself—she squeezed her sweet-smelling baby close to her heart—but she didn't want that for her little son! The emotions of new motherhood were overwhelming her. All she wanted was to protect her child! But if the Roman authorities heard about what had just happened here, how long would it be until they swooped in and killed her baby just as Herod had the innocent children of Bethlehem after the birth of Christ?

"In this age of grace in which we now live, Joanna," her brother-in-law, the bishop of Patara, spoke from her side, "God grants extraordinary blessings to ordinary people. Don't let this great blessing be a cause to weaken your faith."

She turned startled eyes upon him. How did he know what was bothering her?

He continued. "I think He is just telling us that like Paul, when he met the risen Lord on the road to Damascus, your little baby is going to grow up to be a man who will stand on his feet and fight for the people of the world through the Gospel of the Lord."

"To grow up. . ." Joanna grabbed ahold of those blessed words, and when she leaned down to kiss the downy softness of her son's little head, Theophany and his brother exchanged smiles.

They knew that she was just a mother who wanted her child to grow, to have a chance at *life. After the horrors she had experienced in the Roman prison, her fear was understandable.*

Looking up at her brother-in-law, Joanna spoke seriously. "I have been praying to God for this child all my married life, praying that he would be a person who loved the Lord Jesus Christ and would do His will all his long life." A bright smile covered her face as fear released its grip on her soul. "I am thankful for this wonder granted to us—unworthy as we are—by our Lord. I will continue to pray that my son will become a man of God whom God can use."

The Bishop leaned over and kissed his nephew's high forehead. "That is good because this child—all children—need the prayers of their mothers. Against them, Satan has few tools. They are mighty."

※

"Standing" for God is something people of strong faith do. Theophany and Joanna's son standing at an age when it was physically impossible for him to do so showed that they had a big responsibility in bringing up Nicholas. Like Samuel of so long ago, their child was earmarked by God to do great things. But unlike Samuel, who was raised in the tabernacle by the high priest Eli, it was up to their family to raise Nicholas correctly in the knowledge of the Lord.

Nicholas's long life, which included much physical and spiritual warfare against sorcerers, perjurers, and exploiters, proved that through their prayers, Theophany and Joanna succeeded in raising their child right.

Prayer is something especially important for us to keep in mind as this Advent season unfolds and the more secular aspect of the holidays threatens to overtake our time. This Christmas, ask God to keep the glory of Jesus' birth at the center of your celebrations. All prayers throughout the year are good, but most will agree that there is something extra special about Christmastime prayers!

Prepare Your Heart for Christmas

Pick a time of day when you or you and your family can pray, and make it a part of your daily Advent celebration. It's a devotion we can give to God during this time leading up to His day—the birth of His Son!

Please, dear Lord, always let me remember
to come to You in prayer! Amen.

Friendship

Arise, shine; for thy light is come,
*and the glory of the L*ORD *is risen upon thee.*
ISAIAH 60:1 KJV

Do you not know that you are the temple of
God and that the Spirit of God dwells in you?
1 CORINTHIANS 3:16 NKJV

Saint Nicholas was blessed to understand the truth of these verses all his life, including his childhood and adolescent years.

Through prayer, study (he memorized all the scriptures), and self-discipline, Nicholas spent his childhood perfecting his faith. This is one of the reasons he reached such a high level of faith during his life: He never wasted a precious moment.

It wasn't easy. He was a normal boy in all respects. But when it came to friends, he chose very wisely. He didn't want to compromise his faith, or even worse, sadden the Spirit that lived within him.

Eight-year-old Nicholas was waiting at the corner for his father when five boys near his own age swaggered up to him. Nicholas took a deep breath and turned in the opposite direction. He hoped they would walk past him. These boys were like gladiators in training, not kids he wanted to hang out with.

"Well, if it isn't the little scholar boy, Nicholas," the ringleader snarled, forcing Nicholas to face him.

"What do you want, Aristotle?" Nicholas thought it was funny that although this boy shared that great thinker's name, he wasn't anything like the ancient Greek philosopher.

Aristotle flicked his gaze between his followers. He gained strength from their gleaming eyes. He then looked pointedly at Nicholas's sack. "What you got there?" He flicked his finger at the bag.

"My father's lunch, want some?" Nicholas offered but didn't look at Aristotle. He was looking at the tall boy, Pericles, standing in the back. Nicholas had seen Pericles around town before but never as a part of this troublemaking group.

Aristotle yanked the sack from Nicholas's arm. "It's too heavy just for lunch." He ripped the bag open, and when Nicholas's stylus and wax board fell out, he held them up and started dancing around like a monkey. "Hee, hee, hee, can't even leave home without your stylus." The other boys, except for the tall one, all joined in the game.

"Why don't you read what's written on the tablet? If you can read, that is," Nicholas quietly said. These boys played hooky from their lessons more often than they attended.

Aristotle stopped dancing and threw the board to the ground. "I don't want to read your words."

"They're not my words."

Aristotle backed up. "Christian," he jeered, but Nicholas could tell that behind his bravado he was frightened by Who Nicholas represented. "I'm outta here," Aristotle snickered as if Nicholas wasn't worth his valuable time. Turning away, he snapped his fingers for his gang to follow.

They did. Except for Pericles.

Nicholas looked at him.

Pericles offered a tentative smile—the kind a boy gives to another when he really wants to be friends. He reached down and picked up the board and stylus. "Can I read the words?"

"Sure."

" 'Do you not know that you are the temple of God and that the Spirit of God dwells in you?' " The boy seemed to weigh the words before saying "That's. . .nice."

Nicholas nodded. "It is nice."

"I hate the sound of the animals being slaughtered in our temples. I mean, the gods don't even seem to appreciate it. I don't think they care," he said and pointed toward one of the gleaming temples down the street. "Just seems wrong."

"It is wrong," Nicholas said.

Pericles looked down at the sentence Nicholas had copied on his wax board. "Will you tell me about this?"

"Sure."

"We'll have to do it secretly though. My father's a soldier, and he wouldn't like my being around. . .a Christian."

Nicholas put his arm around Pericles's shoulder. "Let me start then by telling you about a man named Nicodemus. . . ."

*

Friendship is one of God's greatest gifts to us.

Singing carols about the Lord's miraculous birth, feasting on tasty food, and celebrating with friends—old and new—during Christmastime are often some of our most treasured moments. That so-called Christmas feeling at its best!

When He walked the earth, Jesus showed how much He valued friendship: He had lots of friends. All saints—people who trust and believe God's Word—are, of course, friends of God. God is within all His saints, so even if we aren't blessed to have close friends among our fellow humans, the relationship we share with God is always on hand to brighten our lives and fill our souls with joy, especially at this time of year. This is the most important friendship we can ever have and the one we are offered because of the very season we now enjoy.

Saint Nicholas guarded his friendship with God above all else and was consequently careful of who he associated with. But he was always prepared to open his heart to those—like Pericles—who wanted to be introduced to his best friend. In fact, introducing others to Jesus was one of Saint Nick's purposes in life!

Prepare Your Heart for Christmas

Is there a person you have often thought about befriending but just haven't had the time? Maybe this Advent season is the time to do so!

Dear Father in heaven, thank You so much for the gift of friendship, especially at Christmastime. And thank You for being my best friend always. Amen.

REPENTANCE

Comfort ye, comfort ye my people, saith your God.
Speak ye comfortably to Jerusalem, and cry unto her, that
her warfare is accomplished, that her iniquity is pardoned.
ISAIAH 40:1–2 KJV

"Take heed that you do not do your charitable deeds before
men, to be seen by them. Otherwise you have no reward from
your Father in heaven. . . . But when you do a charitable deed,
do not let your left hand know what your right hand is doing."
MATTHEW 6:1, 3 NKJV

*A*bout the time when most young men his age
were getting married, Nicholas was ordained a priest.
Shortly afterward his beloved parents died. Feeling
as if their fortune was not his to keep, he prayerfully
sought a way to secretly give it away. He used the
money to change the lives of four people: three sisters
and their desperate father.

"The Three Destitute Maidens" is one of the
best-known stories about Saint Nick. The sisters'

sinful father was about to sell them into slavery in order to pay his creditors when Nicholas stepped in. His generous secret act of giving enabled the young women to marry. Even more, it gave them their father.

Normally this story is told from the standpoint of the sisters. But we will visit it on this, the fourth day of Advent, from the eyes of their father.

"You!" The impoverished merchant shouted out in amazement upon recognizing the young priest that warm summer's eve. He immediately fell face down upon the stones of the residential area at Nicholas's feet.

Nicholas quickly pulled the father of the three girls up. Such regard made him extremely uncomfortable. "You must promise that you won't tell anyone I gave you the gold," Nicholas admonished. Twice before he had tossed a bag of gold through a window of the man's big house. But the merchant had been waiting for him this third time.

The man surprised Nicholas by vigorously nodding his head in agreement. "I will do as you ask. How can I not? You have saved my family." Tears glistened in the older man's eyes.

"I didn't save your family," Nicholas softly corrected. At the man's questioning look he

continued. "I am only a servant of the One who saved your family, the Lord Jesus Christ. All the resources of the earth are His. He is the One who protected your daughters from a father who was so overtaken in his evil life that he could think of such a wicked deed."

The man shuddered at what he'd planned for his daughters. He was going to turn them into prostitutes to pay back his creditors. "Please," the merchant implored, "I beg of you. Tell me, who is this Jesus Christ? I don't want to live another day without getting to know this forgiving God I have ignored all my life." The merchant had reached the lowest level of human dignity.

Since they were close to the man's home, Nicholas led him back to it. They sat together on a bench in the outer courtyard and Nicholas told him about the prophecies of old, about the coming Messiah, the incarnate birth, the Lord's ministry, and His death and resurrection. He told him about the sending of the Holy Spirit and the Church. By the time Nicholas had stopped, the sun was beginning to rise in the eastern sky while the Son of Righteousness had risen within the heart of the man.

"You have not only comforted a lost soul, dear Nicholas of Patara—great servant of the Lord Jesus Christ—but showed me the forgiveness of the Lord with this Good News of *truth. Today I am a repentant man."*

"Now that is a testimony you can tell the people of Patara!" Nicholas exclaimed.

"I will! My heart is no longer weighed down by sin but feels light and free, and I want to tell the whole world about it!"

✳

At Christmastime, this beautiful story is often used as an example of why Nicholas is the model gift giver.

But it's only a small paragraph in the life of this man of faith, and almost insignificant compared to the many other things Nicholas did. It was as a servant of God—a pastor of the people—that Saint Nick gave most to the world. Not just through deeds but in teaching, speaking, and praying.

Young Nicholas knew that the gold was important to this family—as having enough to live on always is. But more than the cash, the real treasure in this heartwarming story was leading the family to their new life in Christ.

Saint Nick gave to the father of the girls the comfort, strength, and peace of mind in the Lord Jesus Christ that enabled him to be made new in Christ. This man's heart had been weighed down with sin. Nicholas led him, through the use of the gift of gold, to the only true freedom there is in the world: faith in the Lord Jesus Christ and His saving work on the cross.

Not one of Nicholas's acts during his lifetime was ever done in the name of "Nicholas." They were all done in the name of the Lord Jesus Christ.

This father saw Jesus in Nicholas's act. The Lord changed this man's heart just as He has been changing hearts every day since His First Advent nearly 2000 years ago!

Prepare Your Heart for Christmas

Do people see the Lord in the acts you perform every day, particularly during the days leading up to Christmas?

Dear God, help me share your love as part of my Christmas activities this year. Amen.

THE EVE OF SAINT NICHOLAS DAY
Archbishop Nicholas of Myra

*For thus saith the LORD of hosts; Yet once, it is a little while,
and I will shake the heavens, and the earth, and the sea,
and the dry land; and I will shake all nations, and the
desire of all nations shall come: and I will fill this
house with glory, saith the LORD of hosts.*
HAGGAI 2:6–7 KJV

*"'And it shall come to pass in the last days, says God,
that I will pour out of My Spirit on all flesh. . .your young
men shall see visions, your old men shall dream dreams.'"*
ACTS 2:17 NKJV

*Let no one despise your youth, but be an
example to the believers in word, in conduct,
in love, in spirit, in faith, in purity.*
I TIMOTHY 4:12 NKJV

*N*icholas had just returned to Asia Minor from
the Holy Land. He'd wanted to stay in the desert

there and, like John the Baptist, live a solitary life. His personal goal was to pray for the world and become as much like Christ as he possibly could.

But this was not what God wanted of him!

It was key that people of faith follow God's leading in their lives so that His "desire of all nations"—that is the building of His Church from among the Gentiles—could come upon the world. God had moved heaven and earth some 272 years earlier with His virgin birth, but now was the glorious time of constructing His Church on earth. Nicholas was to become one of the more splendid weaves in that magnificent fabric (still being woven!) called "Church."

But to be made archbishop of Myra was not something Nicholas wanted!

※

"You are not our choosing, young man, but rather, God's," the elderly bishop told Nicholas. "We bishops of Lycia could not decide who should shepherd the people of the land. We prayed and fasted about it. God told me that whoever entered the church first this morning would be that man."

Dear God, *Nicholas prayed silently.* Was that the reason for the vision? *A few days before Archbishop John of Myra had died, Nicholas had had a dream. In it the Savior stood before him in all His glory and presented Nicholas with a Gospel while his holy mother stood to His right and placed the episcopal cape on Nicholas's shoulders. The vision had stunned Nicholas. He never thought he would be asked to shepherd the souls of men in such a leadership capacity. Never mind Archbishop! It was totally opposite his plans for a private life.*

"Please, tell me, what is your name, young man?" The elderly bishop had been told in his dream the name of the man God had chosen— it was a very unusual name.

"My name is Nicholas, Master. I am your servant."

That was the name!

"Follow me, child," the elderly man requested and led Nicholas to the other bishops, who were still gathered in prayer concerning this important matter. They were overjoyed to meet Nicholas, and when the people of the city heard about him, they all flocked to the church. In spite of his desires for anonymity, many had already heard of the young man, the wonder-worker, Nicholas of Patara.

Nicholas, however, was not at all pleased to be thrust into this position, and if it hadn't been for his extreme faith and the visions given to him by God, he would have walked away from the office. But he did accept. Nicholas knew that it was God's will, and he had learned during his time in the Holy Land that it was much better to change his will and plans than to try and change God's!

This meant that he had to make a major alteration in both his nature and his life plan. Rather than hiding his life from others, he had to open it to all. His life was God's to use.

But how could he fill this role? He was so young!

"'Let no one despise your youth, but be an example to the believers in word, in conduct, in love, in spirit, in faith, in purity,'" Nicholas heard the elderly bishop quote from his side—as if he'd heard his thoughts!

Nicholas looked over at him, and the bishop winked. From that day forward Nicholas was indeed such an example.

❄

Making young Nicholas the archbishop of Myra was just a continuation of the work that God had talked about through the prophet Haggai and which He had started at Pentecost: the building of His Church on earth.

With Nicholas, God took a gentile, whose ancestors had jumped from worshipping idols to worshipping Jesus, and used his faith to continue to build His Church. Nicholas had to radically change his plans for his life—something most people who offer their lives to God are often asked to do. The question is whether a person will accept the change with faith and let God do His will, or not?

Nicholas's life of faith proves that allowing God to lead is always best. Maybe not easy, but best!

Prepare Your Heart for Christmas

Around the world today millions celebrate the 5th of December as the Eve of Saint Nicholas Day. Although its celebration is sometimes made profane by people who abused Nicholas's memory and even worse, that of Christ's, it is important to remember those who protected the Church for us. Can you think of other Christians from the third and fourth centuries who protected the church? This is especially important to remember during these days leading up to the celebration of Christ's Nativity.

Dear Lord, thank You for this time of Advent that reminds us not just of Your coming, but the people of Your Church throughout the ages who have given their lives to You. . .for us. Amen.

December 6

Saint Nicholas Day
The Feast of Saint Nicholas

*For I know that my redeemer liveth, and that he shall stand
at the latter day upon the earth: And though after my skin
worms destroy this body, yet in my flesh shall I see God.*
Job 19:25–26 KJV

*But you have come to Mount Zion and to the city of the
living God. . .to the spirits of just men made perfect, to
Jesus the Mediator of the new covenant, and to the blood of
sprinkling that speaks better things than that of Abel.*
Hebrews 12:22–24 NKJV

Today we will jump ahead to the day that
Nicholas died—December 6, circa AD 345.

Around the world there are many who cherish
the significance of this day and remember it with a
special gladness for Saint Nicholas's Christian witness.
But even when it's not totally remembered why he is
so highly thought of, the fun, if sometimes superficial,

festivities still keep his testimony for Christ from being forgotten.

The Lord of Glory came to His creation as a little baby so that upon our earthly death we could come to "the city of the living God, the heavenly Jerusalem." It is the reason for which salvation—all of the old covenant and the new—was given.

In Saint Nick's case, however, something else rather remarkable occurred.

*

"It was as if angels were singing with the bishops and priests." Sophia softly spoke to her grandmother as they walked with the multitudes away from the church after the funeral service for their beloved archbishop. "Did you hear them, Grandmother?"

"I did." The elderly woman looked around at all the people who, though understanding the joyfulness of the occasion in heaven for the Lord, the angels, and the souls of just men in welcoming Nicholas to his beautiful eternal home, were sad for themselves at losing such a shepherd and teacher. "I think everybody heard the angelic hymns as our dear Nicholas joyfully ascended to heaven. I don't think we could have stood losing him otherwise."

Sophia put her hand into her grandmother's and motioned to all the people who had traveled from far and wide to bid him good-bye. "I don't think so many people have ever been in Myra before."

Grandmother nodded. "He was one of the world's most special people. We are so blessed to have known him personally, to have had him as our leader, our preacher. . . ." Her voice cracked. "Our beloved father."

Sophia reached up and wiped away the tear that had slid down her grandmother's soft cheek. "I felt as if he was always praying for everyone in the world. Even when meeting him on the road, you knew that he was praying. When my parents died," Sophia softly continued, "he came to me during their funeral and told me that I would always be taken care of."

Grandmother bent over and kissed the top of Sophia's sweet-smelling head. She remembered the day after the funeral when he came to their humble house. He had known her greatest fear—that Sophia would be left an orphan. He had assured her that day that she would live to see Sophia to adulthood. Grandmother never doubted his word. "He paid for our house, and there is money set aside for your dowry when the time comes, too."

"Listen to the people, Grandmother," Sophia said. "They are no longer sad and. . . they aren't referring to him as Archbishop Nicholas but as. . .Saint Nicholas!"

Grandmother listened. Sophia was right!
All around people's hearts were gladdened as
they referred to him as saint.

"He was a holy person in life after all,"
Sophia said.

"Even more so now," Grandmother agreed.
"If ever a man lived the victorious Christian life
and was called to be a saint, Saint Nicholas it is
for sure!" She exclaimed and laughed with joy.

Sophia did, too.

❋

The thoughts that must have gone through the
multitude's minds that day in Myra!

Not only had they just lost their beloved and
fearless leader, but all knew that they had been
blessed to know a very special Christian, one who had
accomplished great things for God's Church through
Jesus' name.

Although all New Testament believers are by
grace called *saint* (1 Corinthians 1:2; Ephesians 3:8; 2
Thessalonians 1:10; Jude 3) the church at Nicholas's
time—the same today—did not need to give any
special sanction in order for a person to be called a
saint. Such an honor was by the grace of God and
the recognition of a saintly life by the assembly of
believers. The people were the ones who "canonized"
Nicholas a saint.

He was a friend of God's throughout his entire

life. The life and death of Jesus was the rule by which Nicholas lived all of his ninety-five years.

Is it any wonder that he has been remembered for these last 1700 years. . .especially during this time of the year?

Prepare Your Heart for Christmas

As Christmas approaches, go forward thirty-three years in Christ's life and read the Easter story. They are both part of the greatest story ever told!

Father, please help my faith to grow, especially
now that we are approaching the glorious
celebration of Your birth. Amen.

St Nicholas's Real Elves

*Behold, an angel of the Lord appeared to Joseph in a dream,
saying, "Arise, take the young Child and His mother. . . ."
When he arose, he took the young Child and His
mother by night and departed for Egypt.*
Matthew 2:13–14 nkjv

*So Moses heeded the voice of his father-in-law [Jethro]
and did all that he had said. And Moses chose able men
out of all Israel, and made them heads over the people.*
Exodus 18:24–25 nkjv

We step back again in this Advent journey to
the years after Nicholas, just a young man, was made
archbishop of Myra.

Those thirty-five years could be considered
"silent years" in his life. We aren't told of any specific
events at this time. What we are told however is that
Nicholas was preacher, pastor, overseer—bishop—
extraordinaire! Dimitry of Rostov writes it best in his
"Life of Saint Nicholas": "All day long Nicholas spent

in labor proper to his office, listening to the requests and needs of those who came to him. The doors of his house were open to all. He was kind and affable; to orphans he was a father; to the poor, a merciful giver; to the weeping, a comforter; to the wronged, a helper; and to all, a great benefactor."

Saint Nick is a man who would put secular, modern-day therapists out of work for sure!

But he had learned a wise lesson from his merchantman father and churchman uncle: In order to do the job well that God sets before you, you have to delegate responsibility. Jethro, Moses' father-in-law, had advised his son-in-law about this many centuries earlier. But God had done so just a couple hundred years earlier when He gave Saint Joseph the job of being baby Jesus' human protector. That's delegating on a heavenly scale!

Nicholas knew he had to do the same. But he was new to Myra and didn't know anyone. Who was he to choose?

*

Nicholas was on his knees praying. The care of the metropolis of Myra and all of Lycia—and its organization—was upon him. He had been praying about this great responsibility since his ordination a week ago. Before another day passed he knew that he must find virtuous and wise men who could help him. He felt it would be best if they were men foreign to Myra so the three of them could start from the same position of learning. But how would he find such men?

A knock at his door sounded. Nicholas arose from the floor. The oldest bishop of the land—the one who had been waiting for him at the church the morning he was made archbishop—was there, with two middle-aged men flanking him. Nicholas was pleasantly surprised. He thought all the bishops and priests had returned to their own cities. "Please, sirs, enter." Nicholas stood back for the three to come into the modest house that had belonged to his predecessor.

Without ado the elderly bishop spoke. "Nicholas, I would like to introduce you to Paul of Rhodes and Theodore of Ascalon."

Nicholas's eyes opened wide. He had heard of both men. Their deeds of mercy and kindness were well known throughout the Greco/Roman world. Both were discreet and honorable men. "It is my great pleasure to meet you," Nicholas said and offered them the kiss of peace.

"God has asked me to play Jethro this day, dear Nicholas," the elderly bishop explained the reason for his visit. There was a sparkle in his kind old eyes as he looked between the three men.

Nicholas understood then. He couldn't have been more pleased. "You don't mean. . ." Nicholas took a deep breath. "Does this mean what I think it does?"

"We"—Paul motioned between himself and Theodore—"would be honored if you would consider us as worthy to assist you, Archbishop."

"The honor would be mine, sirs," Nicholas exclaimed. "A most wonderful answer to many nights of prayer. Thank you!" Nicholas looked between them all. "Praise God!" he exclaimed and then laughed, that great big sound of joy that would become famous throughout the decades to come as he and his assistants, all in the name of the babe born in Bethlehem 272 years earlier, brought joy and solace to thousands, nay, to hundreds of thousands!

It's interesting to discover that Saint Nicholas's real "elves" were named Paul and Theodore!

But other than their names, the only thing we know about them is what we read in stories about Saint Nicholas, even though according to Dimitry's *Life*, they were "well known in all of Greece!" In truth, so few Christian men and women *are* remembered past a few generations.

These two men were fine pastors and counselors who assisted Nicholas in becoming the great leader he was to become throughout the next years. Except for their relationship to Nicholas they would have remained unnamed saints to history. People such as

Paul and Theodore can be seen today as the secretaries, choir masters, youth leaders, deacons, and volunteers who help leaders like Nicholas to successfully follow the vocation God has called them to.

Helpers are vital to God's work. Jethro knew Moses needed to delegate responsibility in the forming of the first nation of Israel. But even more, God trusted the human protector of His Son, Joseph, so greatly that He gave over the care of His only begotten Son to that humble man as the second Israel, based on grace, was formed.

Nicholas of Myra was wisely following good examples.

Prepare Your Heart for Christmas

How can we be "elves" and assist our pastors and priests, especially during this very wonderful, but busy, time of year?

Heavenly Father, help me to be a helper to all whose paths cross mine during these lovely, but hectic, days of Advent. Amen.

Fear Not

Why do the nations conspire and the peoples plot in vain?
The kings of the earth rise up and the rulers band together
against the LORD and against his anointed.
PSALM 2:1–2 NIV

And the angel said unto them, Fear not.
LUKE 2:10 KJV

The seventy-two returned with joy and said, "Lord,
even the demons submit to us in your name." He replied,
"I saw Satan fall like lightning from heaven."
LUKE 10:17–18 NIV

For eight years Saint Nicholas was imprisoned for being a Christian. He suffered all kinds of terrible discomforts, even torture.

What did this now middle-aged man do? Did he renounce Christ and encourage others to do so, too, saying God would understand. . . ? Of course not: He wouldn't have been our beloved Saint Nicholas if he had!

He continued to bravely proclaim the Gospel of Christ. He preached how the evil going on in the world wasn't God's doing any more than evil ever is. That all that is true and noble, just and pure, lovely and admirable, excellent and praiseworthy however, was, is, and always will be from God (Philippians 4:8). God wasn't to be slandered!

Because of people like Nicholas, there were plenty of wonderful things happening in the Empire, too. Christian prayers were being said by the millions. Prayers that would end up changing the world! When a leader such as Nicholas is around to faithfully feed people the Word, sing the Gospel truth, and remember the holy days of God, the evils of the world eventually have to "fall like lightning from heaven" (Luke 10:18).

Let's take a glimpse into the seventh Nativity that Nicholas celebrated with his fellow Christian inmates. He had been warned by the new and vicious captain of the Roman guard that if he told the Nativity story, he would be taken and punished. This point in his life could be considered sad. But as with Good Friday, it's actually victorious!

*

Nicholas had just finished offering the liturgical praise service to the Lord. He was now sitting among his congregation in the dank, dark prison. But somehow with their archbishop present, the unheated stone room felt warm and cozy. Besides, today Archbishop Nicholas was going to retell the Lord's Nativity story!

Young and old sat nestled together in rapt expectation of his words. Even though all scriptures had been destroyed, their beloved archbishop could remember every word.

"'It came to pass. . . ,'" his melodious voice began. All were transported away from the prison to that most blessed time. "'That there went out a decree from Caesar Augustus. . .that all. . . should be taxed. . . .'" He spoke slowly so no one missed a word. "'And Joseph also went. . .to. . . Bethlehem. . .with Mary. . . And so it was that. . . the days were accomplished that she should be delivered.'"

Smiles covered all faces. They knew what was coming but savored it as if it were a first-time hearing. "'And she brought forth her firstborn son.'" A combined sigh filled the room. Nicholas's eyes twinkled out over them all before he continued. "'Now there were. . .shepherds . . .in the fields. . . And behold, an angel of the Lord stood before them and the glory of the Lord shone around them. . .they were greatly afraid—'"

"Priest!" The harsh voice of the captain of the guard barked out. Everyone jumped. "I warned you not to tell that story today!" The

captain was in a rage and having a hard time opening the lock on the cell.

All were terrified and huddled closer together. But not Nicholas. Standing, he continued the Nativity story as if the irate captain hadn't intruded on their moment. "'Fear not,'" Nicholas's voice crescendoed as he chanted out the angel's most glorious line, "'for behold, I bring you good tidings of great joy which will be to all people. For there is born to you this day in the city of David a Savior, who is Christ the Lord!'" Victorious words!

But having opened the gate, the captain rushed forward, grabbed Nicholas by his beard, and yanked him violently to his knees. All cried out in anguish for their beloved leader. "You will pray you never spoke today, Priest," the captain ground out.

"No, sir," Nicholas said, even though his physical pain was great. "This is the one day of the year that I will always pray to speak!"

❄

If ever a prayer was answered it was that one!

No man has ever "spoken" more loudly each and every year at Christmastime than he! Maybe not in the way he would have envisioned—through his current alter ego, Santa Claus—but in a way that has reverberated with joy and gladness down through the centuries.

His most important message, of course, is to remind all that, no matter our circumstances, we must always remember when God was born in Bethlehem, totally human while still being totally God!

The angel told the shepherds to "fear not."

That was a command Saint Nick lived his life by.

Prepare Your Heart for Christmas

Do we take the scriptures for granted? Make memorizing the Christmas story part of your celebration this year (Luke 2:1–20; Matthew 1:18–2:18). That way, Christ's Nativity will always be in your hearts, and like Saint Nick, you'll always have it available to retell!

Dear Lord, thank You, thank You,
thank You for taking on flesh. . .to save me!
Amen.

Bethlehem. . .
Once Again Good Tidings!

Arise, shine; for thy light is come, and the glory of the
LORD is risen upon thee. . . . And the Gentiles shall come
to thy light, and kings to the brightness of thy rising.
Isaiah 60:1, 3 KJV

For, behold, I bring you good tidings of
great joy, which shall be to all people.
Luke 2:10 KJV

Nicholas had finally been let out of prison
when he was about sixty-one years old. He had been
tortured for his faith and was now about a third his
normal size. His congregation, being very worried
about him, decided that the best way to keep their
beloved archbishop with them was to send him away.
He needed rest and protection from the fickle and
fanatical pagan emperor, Maximian Daia, who now
ruled the land of Asia Minor. Knowing how special
the Nativity of Christ was to Nicholas, they secretly

sent him to the safety of a retreat that was located close to Bethlehem in the bordering town of Beit Jala.

Nicholas gratefully went. His body had reached its limit, and even though he'd initially wanted to live in the Holy Land in solitude, he now desired more than anything to regain his strength and be with his congregation.

He went to Beit Jala to rest, but mostly to pray for the empire.

It is now Christmas Eve, and Nicholas has just been reunited with his old childhood friend, Pericles. He receives from this old Roman soldier a firsthand account that is almost as astounding as that given by the angels to the shepherds on the Bethlehem hills!

✳

"I was there and saw it," Pericles assured Nicholas.

"Bless you, my dear old friend, for coming and telling me yourself." There were tears in Nicholas's eyes, both at seeing Pericles again and for his news. "Tell me again what happened."

Pericles gladly did so. "The sun had just passed noon. We were camped nine miles north of Rome. Suddenly, a light, cutting all across the sky shone above the sun. It was a cross. The soldiers—pagans most—were terrified. They thought it meant that they would all die in battle. But our emperor, Constantine, wasn't afraid. He stood tall and looked at the sight in a way that made me sure that he was one of us, Nicholas—a Christian!"

"I have often wondered about him," Nicholas confessed. "His father, Constantius, was most likely a Christian. But privately."

"Well, Constantine is now a very public one! He gazed at the sign of the cross fearlessly all afternoon. There was adoration in his eyes. He knew it was a trophy, something to be cherished."

"And that night our Lord came to him in a dream and told him to have a cross painted on the shields: That by that sign he would conquer?" Nicholas prodded.

"Exactly! We did so, and Constantine's troops freed Rome. But most important of all, that day Constantine showed openly to the world that he is a Christian!"

Nicholas turned and looked out over the hills of Bethlehem, the very same where the best news of all—the coming of the Messiah—had been given by angels to men.

" 'Kings shall come to your light, and the Gentiles to your brightness,' " he softly quoted from Isaiah. " 'The wealth. . .of nations and peoples shall change their course and turn to you.' "

"That is exactly what is happening!" Pericles exclaimed. "The Emperor Constantine has come to the light of the Lord!"

Nicholas took his tall soldier friend by his upper arms and gave him a happy shake. "The world is about to change, Pericles, in a most magnificent way!"

"In the way the Lord had it planned since first He came here," Pericles looked out over Bethlehem. "Just a little baby."

"Amen!" Nicholas agreed and then laughed, a great and jovial sound that hadn't been heard since before the persecution. "We are in Bethlehem and once again, good tidings!"

"It's the best tribute to Christ's birth since the very first," Pericles agreed.

✳

The "good tidings of great joy" proclaimed by the angels singing in the Bethlehem sky was echoed when the light of the cross shone against the sky for Constantine and his thousands of soldiers. For the first time since the coming of the Holy Spirit at Pentecost, Christianity was accepted by the leader of a powerful government—the Roman Empire!

This time the news was being heralded by Christian soldiers such as Pericles, who came from lands all across the empire. Soldiers returned to their homelands and told the account of the miraculous, "Cross in the Sky," and about the great emperor of the West, Constantine, who heard God's call. Being a good and faithful servant, Constantine immediately set about using his position of authority to change the course of the world. Soon, Constantine would loudly proclaim Jesus Christ from his throne.

Nicholas suspected that great things were about to happen. This Christmas was a very happy one for him.

Prepare Your Heart for Christmas

Consider this Christmas season how you might feel if you had your Bible, church, family, and friends all taken away from you, but then, through a miracle of God, a politician came to power who, understanding the Gospel message, changed the world!

> *Dear God, help me never to take the*
> *celebration of Your birth for granted.*
> *Amen.*

FREEDOM IN CHRIST

*"Break down their altars, smash their sacred
stones and cut down their Asherah poles."*
EXODUS 34:13 NIV

*And Jesus rebuked the demon. . . Then the disciples came to
Jesus privately and said, "Why could we not cast it out?". . .
"Because of your unbelief; for assuredly, I say to you, if you
have faith as a mustard seed, you will say to this mountain,
'Move from here to there,' and it will move; and nothing
will be impossible for you. However, this kind does not
go out except by prayer and fasting."*
MATTHEW 17:18–21 NKJV

*N*icholas was right. Great things were indeed
unfolding in the world! They had been since that first
Christmas Day. Now a great leap toward the freedom
only to be found in Christ was being backed by the
first openly Christian emperor.

In April of 313 the Roman emperor of the West,
Constantine, drafted an amazing document—the

Edict of Milan. For the first time in history, religious freedom was granted to *all*.

A decade later, Constantine was the sole ruler of the Roman Empire. Christianity was *not* the religion of the empire, but it was now the favored one by this believing emperor.

All these political events affected Nicholas's life greatly.

Nicholas returned to Myra and shepherded the Christians of his land. By the grace of Jesus, he went about delivering *all* the people from the false and materialistic ways of the temples, such as those Paul fought against in Acts 19. But now, unlike Paul, Nicholas would not be imprisoned or killed for preaching God and telling the truth about "gods and goddesses." Not even when by Nicholas's prayers to the Lord Jesus Christ and his faith—which by this time had grown to be a perfect combination of belief and trust—those temples toppled to the ground!

Seventy-four-year-old Nicholas had spent the last forty days in prayer and fasting. Like Paul long before him, he was soon to battle one of the most skilled deceivers.

During the last few years he had bravely taken on many of the pagan temples in his city that were inhabited by the Greek, Roman, and Egyptian "gods"—demons actually. In this time of grace people had the weapons, authority, knowledge, and commission—the name of the Lord Jesus Christ—to fight against the Prince of Darkness. Nicholas knew that there was no excuse for him not to set free his countrymen from this deception. Fear used to grip him when he passed by the demons' domiciles. Not any longer.

Many of the city's temples had been cleansed of the unclean spirits through the faith of Saint Nicholas. People had even heard the bad spirits fleeing and crying at their misfortune to have come up against such a mighty servant of God.

But to fight Artemis (Diana) was an extreme test even for Nicholas. One he hadn't felt prepared to take on—until now.

As he walked toward the temple—with his robes billowing around him—he was deep in prayer. The multitude of faithful in Myra walked with him, all praying for their archbishop and for God to do a great wonder this day through his—and their—faith. The Christians of Myra had tasted spiritual freedom, and they wanted the same for all their countrymen and people everywhere. It was something they knew their archbishop, through the Lord Jesus Christ, could give them.

Nicholas stopped before the edifice built in the "goddess's" honor. The building shuddered like in an earthquake. But it wasn't the earth *that was causing it to move, rather it was Nicholas's faith.*

With a clear and fearless voice he spoke to the spirits within the building. "The Lord God Almighty did not condescend to come to earth as a little baby and then thirty-three years later suffered crucifixion so that evil spirits may continue to enslave His people and inhabit some of humankind's most beautiful structures! In the Lord Jesus Christ's name, I command you. . .be gone from this building!"

The response was immediate. At the name of Jesus, it couldn't be otherwise!

The sound of the unholy altars crashing to the ground filled the air.

The idols—statues in the so-called likeness of Artemis—fell forward onto their faces. Dust rose up and around the building, making it look like a newly cut tomb.

Satan, the ancient deceiver of men, could not stand before the Lord Jesus Christ!

Wow!

This might seem like the prelude to a Hollywood blockbuster. But it's actually nothing of the kind. It's truth. This is one of the many things Saint Nick did through his faith in God. It's actually another reason why Nicholas is considered the ultimate gift giver. One of the greatest gifts he gave was the knowledge and example that through faith in Jesus, freedom from slavery to sin and false worship can be everybody's throughout the world.

Even by our modern standards Nicholas would be considered an older gentleman now.

But this is only day ten of the Advent count-down. Including Christmas Day we have fifteen more days to go!

Saint Nicholas did his most amazing work during his "senior years"!

Prepare Your Heart for Christmas

Does your faith in God and His gifts to us move mountains? It can! During these glorious days of Advent think how.

> *Dear Lord in heaven, please increase my faith*
> *so that I may move "mountains" as your servant,*
> *Nicholas of Myra, did. Amen.*

SON OF GOD

For unto us a Child is born, unto us a Son is given;
and the government will be upon His shoulder.
And His name will be called Wonderful, Counselor,
Mighty God, Everlasting Father, Prince of Peace.
ISAIAH 9:6 NKJV

Joseph said to them, "Do not be afraid. . .you meant evil
against me; but God meant it for good, in order to bring
it about as it is this day, to save many people alive."
GENESIS 50:19–20 NKJV

Then Jesus went into the temple of God and drove out all
those who bought and sold in the temple. . . . And He said
to them, "It is written, 'My house shall be called a house of
prayer,' but you have made it a 'den of thieves.'"
MATTHEW 21:12–13 NKJV

*E*mperor Constantine summoned a council of the church in 325. The Council of Nicaea was called to settle a dispute that was raging within the church.

Saint Nick attended this council as one of the

318 bishops. Similar to Jesus when He cleansed the temple, he made quite an impression on everyone! No one expects holy people to ever get angry. But the instigator of this controversy, the priest Arius, did anger Nicholas.

*

Wack!

The sound reverberated around the vast hall and was quickly followed by a gasp from the thousand or so churchmen in attendance.

Nicholas of Myra had slapped the priest Arius on his smirking face. The majority of those present agreed with the archbishop though. After hours of having Arius monopolize the meeting with his arguments, lies, and slander against the Lord Jesus, they had all wanted to do the same. Arius was teaching false ideas around the world. Most realized he only wanted fame and glory for himself and his party. They were trying to hijack the truth about the nature of Christ—to steal real knowledge of Him from future generations of people.

When Nicholas opened his mouth to speak, all listened—even their emperor, Constantine, who had convened this council. "To say that Jesus—the Son of God—is a creature and a work of God and that there was a time when He did not exist and that He is not of the same substance as the Father. . . . You are not a friend

*of God, Arius. Rather you are worse than the
pagans with their terrible animal sacrifices and
immoral living. You are trying to destroy the
Church from within."*

*Nicholas paused and looked the cowering
priest up and down. Everyone knew that
Nicholas's faith had accomplished amazing
wonders. Arius was right to be afraid. "You may
think you are winning—your party might even
rally for a few years—but God is in control. Just
as with Joseph, whose brothers sold him into
slavery, God will use your evil lies, Arius, for the
betterment of all people."*

*Nicholas turned to the emperor and said,
"Great things will come from this council, sir."*

*Finished, Nicholas bowed to the emperor,
whom he greatly respected.*

*Then he waited for what might come.
Nicholas knew that to strike a person in the
presence of the emperor was punishable by
cutting off the hand.*

He was prepared to pay the price.

*That's why he had used his left hand. It was
expendable. With his right hand he served the
Lord. He flexed the muscles in his left hand and
prayed that he might not have to pay such a
dear price for speaking the truth. . . .*

❋

His prayer was answered.

Constantine gave the matter over to the bishops in the hall. None wanted Nicholas maimed for doing what they'd all wanted to do. Neither did the emperor (who had been writing laws to rid the world of such terrible pagan laws). They recommended that Nicholas be dismissed from the council and imprisoned. Constantine was relieved to agree with this more minor sentence.

But God had other plans! Soon Nicholas was not only released but even the emperor himself begged Nicholas's pardon—as did the other churchmen of the council!

Nicholas was doing God's will by proclaiming the Son of God before Arius and all the bishops of the empire.

When Isaiah wrote the words, "For unto us a Child is born, unto us a Son is given; and the government will be upon His shoulder. And His name will be called Wonderful, Counselor, Mighty God, Everlasting Father, Prince of Peace," it had been a prophecy.

It no longer was. Christ had come to earth three centuries earlier!

God used something intended for bad—Arius's insults against Christ—for good. From this council we get the first part of the Nicene Creed!

Prepare Your Heart for Christmas

Consider how God has protected His Church—and the celebration of Christmas—through the Nicene Creed. The first part will be 1700 years old in 2025. Do you know it by heart? *"I believe in one God, the Father Almighty, Maker of heaven and earth, and of all things visible and invisible, and in one Lord, Jesus Christ, the Only-begotten Son of God, begotten of the Father before all ages. Light of Light, true God of true God, begotten not made. Of one essence with the Father, through whom all things were made. Who for us men and for our salvation came down from heaven, and was incarnate of the Holy Spirit and of the Virgin Mary, and became man."*

> *Heavenly Father, thank You for saintly men and women down through the centuries who have protected the Gospel truth for. . .me. Amen.*

IMPERIAL BANQUET

*The coastlands saw it and feared, the ends of the earth
were afraid; they drew near and came. Everyone helped
his neighbor, and said to his brother, "Be of good courage!"
So the craftsman encouraged the goldsmith; he who smooths
with the hammer inspired him who strikes the anvil,
saying, "It is ready for the soldering"; then he fastened
it with pegs, that it might not totter.*

ISAIAH 41:5–7 NKJV

*And it came to pass in those days, that there went out a decree
from Caesar Augustus, that all the world should be taxed.*

LUKE 2:1 KJV

The council was over.

All the churchmen—including Saint Nicholas—
made ready to return to their homes.

But the palace was abuzz. The emperor was
throwing a party!

Although there were public festivals all over the
empire in honor of Constantine's twentieth year on

the throne, the emperor had his own ideas on how he wanted to celebrate. Constantine wanted to give thanks to God. But even more, he wanted to do so with the men whose faith and will had just finished a mighty work.

Nicholas understood that in a very unselfish move, this wise emperor didn't want to celebrate his personal victory in achieving twenty years in power, but rather the greatest victory of all—the Church that was "ready for the soldering." It was an unmatched occasion.

But Nicholas thought it was exactly what should have been ordered by Caesar Augustus when Jesus was born 329 years earlier. Instead, that emperor had ordered "all world taxed!" Constantine was correcting that mistake. He was celebrating the Great "I Am's" birth, and even more, the Church that Jesus had willingly bought with His sacrifice.

Let's join Nicholas as he entered that feast.

❋

Sure enough, the greatest hall in the land was prepared. A large Roman guard was stationed with drawn swords. The emperor's very special guests were now being protected by the very guards who had imprisoned them just a few years earlier!

Nicholas noticed that even the emperor's bodyguards were present at this event.

Constantine hadn't allowed them at the council, deeming God's protection enough. But this was a banquet. The emperor had many enemies who didn't like him leaving the old pagan ways and becoming Christian.

Nicholas glanced to his left and gasped.

The Roman commander who had broken up his reading of the Nativity story stood there. He was glowering at Nicholas.

A chill ran down Nicholas's spine. This man was no Christian.

Nicholas's respect for Constantine grew even greater. Even with the majority of his soldiers being pagan, the emperor was still doing God's will on earth to the best of his human abilities.

Nicholas bowed his head in the guard's direction while within himself he prayed, Save, O Lord, and have mercy upon this guard who hates me so. Do not let him perish through me, a sinner. *Nicholas hoped that he would see this soldier in glory someday.*

Glory. . .

That was what Nicholas felt he was beholding a few moments later when he entered the private imperial apartment where the banquet was being held.

Splendor shone all around. It was as if the very light of God lit the space. "'The Lamb is its light,'" Nicholas spoke the words about the New Jerusalem from Revelation 21.

*The Roman representative to Nicaea,
Vito, nodded his head. "You are so correct,
Archbishop." Nicholas smiled over at the young
man who was walking beside him.*

*"I am sure it is still only a pale shadow of
that real glory," Vito said. "But Constantine
is honoring our Lord's Church by hosting this
banquet in such a style. Never have kings of
nations been treated more grandly, let alone
priests. God is working in him to do great things."*

*"Amen." Nicholas could only agree as he
looked at their host—the Roman emperor who
invited churchmen to celebrate his twentieth
anniversary with him! Amazing! "With God all
things truly are possible," he said and laughed
out loud.*

*"Yes, Archbishop." Vito chuckled in
agreement. "Truly it is so!"*

❋

Is it any wonder Constantine is called, "the Great"?

For the first time in history the ruler of the entire
western world had taken up the banner of Christ. It
was the start of monarchs who would give the Church
their protection. Evil and incompetent kings might
come and go—and people might slander it and try to
rewrite what really happened—but the Church would
survive because of men of faith such as Nicholas,
Constantine, and Vito.

But this would never have happened if God hadn't sent His Son as a baby. All of history—and our futures—goes back to the birth of Jesus Christ!

The banquet that should have been given in honor of Christ's birth by the first emperor of the Roman Empire was finally given by the first *Christian* emperor of the Roman Empire, Constantine!

And Nicholas of Myra—well, he was invited!

Prepare Your Heart for Christmas

Just imagine if Caesar Augustus had given a banquet in Jesus' honor as Constantine the Great did years later! How different might the world be today if he had?

Dear Father, blessed is Your name!
Thank You for miracles that are all around us. . .
even those we often overlook, such as this
beautiful banquet that finally took place! Amen.

PAPOULI

All your children shall be taught by the LORD,
and great shall be the peace of your children.
ISAIAH 54:13 NKJV

"The King will reply, 'Truly I tell you, whatever
you did for one of the least of these brothers
and sisters of mine, you did for me.'"
MATTHEW 25:40 NIV

Glory to God in the highest, and on
earth peace, good will toward men.
LUKE 2:14 KJV

Peace and *good will*. . .

Two words that bring to mind feelings of
warmth, joy, kindness, love, friendship, rest, family,
and of course, children with happy faces!

The period after the council was a peaceful time
for the Church. It was a time to proclaim without fear
the saving life of Christ! A time to rejoice that relief

had finally come to the Church. It was a rest from political tyranny: For the first time in history the pagan world wasn't allowed to persecute and enslave the population that worshipped Jesus!

Next we take a break with Saint Nicholas as we experience with him this lovely time. We can almost feel his relief. We must enjoy it though because, as is often the case, such "golden" times don't last long in this sin-infected world. Soon, Saint Nicholas's work would once more become intense. But for a few years, because of living under such a wise ruler, he had time to enjoy the people of Myra and none more than the children he loved so much. He could even indulge in his favorite hobbies.

What were they?

Toy and book making, of course!

❋

It was a sweet summer's eve and all the orphaned children were gathered in the courtyard under the cool leaves of the giant plane tree.

But it wasn't because of the adorable kittens that frolicked around the children that they were so excited. It was because they were waiting for their very own Papouli—little grandfather—to come.

He entered and their eyes turned wide as saucers, especially when they saw the sack he had slung over his back.

All knew what that meant!

Books and toys!

They all wanted to run up to their dear
Papouli and throw their arms around him. But
until they were given permission to move, none
did, not even the smallest of them, little Maria.

Bishop Nicholas sat down on the bench,
the same one he always sat on, smiled at them,
placed his sack behind him, and then opened
his arms wide.

"Papouli!" the children sang out, and
with laughter and happy sounds they descended
upon him!

None laughed more loudly and gleefully
than the old bishop himself!

To visit these dear little ones who had lost
all their relatives was Nicholas's favorite thing to
do. He wished he could adopt every child. But
he knew he couldn't do that. . . .

But he could be a grandfather to them all!

He could make sure none ever wanted for
any necessity. He could even, he thought as he
reached behind him and pulled his sack up
front, give them some fun things, too.

From the youngest to the oldest, each child
would receive a present from his own hands. Toy
making had been a hobby he had learned from
his mother, book making from his uncle. Any
spare time he had was spent making things for
children.

"Let's see," he said as he rummaged around in his sack. "Ah yes, Maria." He looked at the little girl who had the saddest eyes he had ever seen. Softly he said, "I have this little doll here." He pulled the toy out of his sack, and all the children gasped in appreciation of its beauty. "She really needs a mommy to love her. Would you like to be this little doll's mommy?" he asked as he handed the doll to Maria.

Her eyes brightened as she hugged the doll close to her heart with one arm and threw the other around Nicholas's neck. "Thank you, Papouli! I will love it forever! And you, too!"

Nicholas kissed the happy child on her forehead. "And I will love you, Maria, and all the children in the world for always, too," he vowed.

*

That was a promise Saint Nicholas has certainly kept!

Any person—both young and old—who God brought into Nicholas's path never went without the basic necessities. But even more, his attitude of love was something people throughout the ages would start to emulate. Because of Nicholas's example, as well as the political climate brought about by the first Christian emperor, the world started to care for those in unfortunate circumstances, understanding that to do so was to do for Christ Himself.

Saint Nick has continued, even if many only see him in his alter ego of Santa Claus! Never more than during Advent are we aware of his continued "presence" in our lives.

Prepare Your Heart for Christmas

Who do you know that might be considered "one of the least of these brothers and sisters of mine," that you might help during this Advent season? Remember, by "doing" for that person you are "doing" for Jesus.

Please, Lord, help me, like Saint Nicholas, to always see Your face in the face of my brothers and sisters who now walk the earth with me. Help me never to miss a chance to "do" for another. Amen.

THE CITY OF THE LORD

"The sons of foreigners shall build up your walls, and their
kings shall minister to you. . .that men may bring to you the
wealth of the Gentiles, and their kings in procession. . . .
And they shall call you The City of the LORD."
ISAIAH 60:10, 11, 14 NKJV

By faith Abraham obeyed. . .for he waited for the city which
has foundations, whose builder and maker is God.
HEBREWS 11:8, 10 NKJV

May 11, 330: What a magnificent day in
history.

It was the day when the very first city *ever* was
dedicated to the Lord Jesus Christ and His saving
work on the cross: the city that was to be known as
Constantinople.

What a city!

But Constantinople was not its original name.
Constantine did not dedicate the city to himself, but
rather he christened it "New Rome." The emperor

knew that in order for the empire to survive in our world so infiltrated by sin that it had to have as its foundation Christ. He was in a position to change things. Because of his rank, and his personal decision to believe Christ, he stood accountable before the Lord Jesus Christ to do so. He built this great city in answer to that call.

We come to the day in the life of Nicholas of Myra when the newest capital of the empire—New Rome—was dedicated. It is doubtful that it was an event this sailor of the seas would have missed!

❄

The day was as beautiful and fresh as only May days could be in the ancient Greek town of Byzantium.

Nicholas was one of thousands who had travelled to the Straights of the Bosporus to be present when the newest city to become an imperial capital was dedicated by the emperor himself.

"Did you know that Troy had been considered as a possible location for the emperor's new capital?" Petros, the son of Nicholas's childhood friend Pericles asked from his side. The old soldier, Pericles, had long since passed on to eternity. His son, Petros, a priest in Patara, often accompanied Nicholas on his journeys.

"Yes, but our fine emperor considers this location to be as close to the center of the world as possible, and as such better to spread the Gospel of Christ."

Petros nodded and looked around. "This peninsula is not only beautiful but strategic." He pointed toward the southwest. "The Sea of Marmara is there and it connects with the Aegean Sea." Pointing to the northeast. "The Bosporus there, connecting to the Black Sea, while the Golden Horn"—he indicated north to the inlet and natural harbor of Byzantium—"makes this such a special and tactical peninsula."

Nicholas chuckled. "Well, when the Greek from Megara, Byzas, first settled in this unclaimed land nearly a thousand years ago, he considered his countrymen to have been blind"—he pointed to Chalcedon on the opposite shore—"to not have built here."

"Constantine has certainly corrected that mistake!" Petros exclaimed. "Did you hear the story of the marking of the city's limits in November of 326?"

Nicholas knew it but never tired of hearing it. "Tell me."

"Constantine walked and walked for what seemed like miles. When one of his generals ventured to ask, 'Sire, where are you taking us? You are making the walls of the city too big.'

"'I can't stop,' the emperor had said. 'Someone else is leading me on.'"

Nicholas and Petros smiled. They had no doubt about the invisible Someone's identity! Others might wonder in the future, but Saint Nicholas and his friend Petros knew who the real builder behind this, the world's first Christian city, really was! The beautiful edifice dedicated to the holy Trinity proclaimed it, and the even larger cathedral dedicated to Holy Wisdom (Saint Sophia) was under construction behind them.

"'A city that is set on a hill cannot be hidden,'" Nicholas murmured. There were tears in his eyes for this first Christian city; something that could never be taken from it nor the ministry of Constantine.

When did "New Rome" get the name "Constantinople"? The emperor was so loved that after his death everyone referred to the city as Constantinople—the City of Constantine, the man who loved Jesus.

It was a great honor to be sure, but made more so because this city was Constantine's personal gift to God's Son. The wise Gentile kings from the *East* offered gold, frankincense, and myrrh to the newborn Lord. This wise Gentile king from the *West* offered this city to the risen Christ.

What a city!

As is to be expected of a city that was built in Jesus' honor, this one was more beautiful and prosperous than any other. This "Queen of Cities" soon became known simply as "*The* City." Even its modern name, Istanbul, refers back to the three Greek words "*Is tin Poli*" meaning, "To *The* City."

But the day that the city was dedicated to the Lord Jesus Christ was a first for the world.

With it, the highest official in the Roman Empire—one of the most powerful political entities in history—proclaimed that The City set upon these hills belonged to the Light of the World, the Lord Jesus Christ.

Now that's a pretty amazing gift to give the risen Lord—one the Wise men would most definitely approve!

Prepare Your Heart for Christmas

Consider this Advent season how we might make our own city—or home—as one offered to God.

God, please help me to remember those who lived before me who, understanding their accountability before You, bravely brought forward a world in which You reign. Help me to be like them. Amen.

No Food for Advent?

He tends his flock like a shepherd: He gathers the
lambs in his arms and carries them close to his heart;
he gently leads those that have young.
ISAIAH 40:11 NIV

"As the heavens are higher than the earth,
so are my ways higher than your ways."
ISAIAH 55:9 NIV

"And do not set your heart on what you will eat or drink; do
not worry about it. For the pagan world runs after all such
things, and your Father knows that you need them. But seek
his kingdom, and these things will be given to you as well."
LUKE 12:29–31 NIV

*F*or some, to not have all the delicacies we
associate with the Advent season isn't such a hardship.
Millions of Christians around the world fast (both an
inner fast of the heart to accompany the outward fast
of food) for forty days preceding the Feast of Christ's

Nativity. It is a time of introspection, compassion, and prayer to prepare for the Lord's arrival. For those Christians, the feasting begins with the first day of Christmas—Christmas Day! But even for those who fast, to have no food at all is not a situation anyone would want to find themselves in.

This is what the people of Myra experienced when a great famine struck the land.

Being a great leader of the church and a man who, like the Christians who came before him, fasted often, Nicholas understood well that we rely on God for our physical health and safety. It's only indirectly dependent on food, clothing, and shelter. Anxiety over any sort of physical need is showing a lack of faith in God's provision. But Saint Nicholas also felt pity for the people of his city. He also knew that not everyone's faith could survive a lack of food. He prayed to God that he could do something directly about this great need his flock was experiencing.

*

Jubilation abounded in Myra. A ship laden with grain from Egypt had arrived and was selling wheat to the hungry inhabitants.

"It's you!" the captain of the vessel shouted out and pointed at Archbishop Nicholas when he walked to the main square in the agora.

"You came to me while I was sleeping and told me to bring my cargo here, that I would be well

paid for my trouble."

"Have you been?" Nicholas asked. There was a twinkle in his eye that all the people of Myra knew meant something extraordinary was up. They knew that their archbishop had to somehow be behind this miraculous turn of events. All ships from Egypt passed by Myra, needing to keep the hungry mouths of Italy and Gaul well fed. The Goths had ravaged the land to the north and even New Rome—Constantinople—was in need because of the lack of working farmlands. Myra would normally be one of the last cities to be sold much-needed grain.

The captain nodded his head and pulled out from his pouch three gold coins. "You didn't just come to me in my dream—you left me these."

The crowd gasped.

"They're gold. . ."

"They're real. . ."

"Gold coins. . .being left through a dream?"

The people turned to their archbishop. They were used to wonders being performed through the faith of their leader, but this was something extraordinary.

"You would not have come without that deposit," Nicholas answered simply. "The people of Myra need your grain."

"But. . ."

"Do not question God's ways," Nicholas

*reprimanded. But then, with that playful
twinkle in his giving eyes continued with "or
those of His servants. God's ways are so much
higher than our own."*

"But. . ."

*"In these glorious days in which we now
live"—Nicholas turned to include all the people
gathered around as he gave an impromptu
sermon—"never forget, my dear ones, that God
is with us. God can do whatever He wants to
do. Great wonders or small, they are all the
same to Him." His smile deepened and his eyes
sparkled even more. "And really, next to His
Birth and Resurrection isn't a ship full with
grain arriving in our port just a very small
miracle?"*

*When put like that the people couldn't help
but agree. When one person in the crowd started
singing "Glory to God in the Highest," all soon
joined in.*

*Even the merchant and his sailors whose faith
had been strengthened a thousandfold that day.*

*And of course, Archbishop Nicholas. He
sang the loudest of all!*

※

It was a good day for the people of Myra. . .and for
the people of the world who would hear about the
Account of the Famine.

By this time in Saint Nicholas's life his fame—

what he'd never wanted—was well known around the world. His action at the Council of Nicaea alone would have given him such notoriety. It's very likely that the captain of the ship knew about him so when the gold coins showed up in his cabin that captain knew better than not to heed the command!

But it is Nicholas's response that we should remember. Nicholas never ever did anything for his own glory, but for the glory of God so that his life would witness to the saving grace of Christ.

He was wise enough to know that one of the best ways to do that was to answer the call of his parishioners' bellies. To be well fed is one of God's greatest blessings to His children.

Prepare Your Heart for Christmas

Consider the food you eat today and during Advent. Maybe choose one day—just one day—to eat half of your normal amount to get an idea of what a magnificent blessing it is to have food—delicious and tasty food at that!—sitting on our tables each day to satisfy our hunger.

Note: Only do this exercise if there are no food-related disorders in your family.

Faith, Lord, faith! Please strengthen mine today so that when your Second Advent comes, I will be well prepared. Amen.

BEAUTIFUL FEET

*How then shall they call on Him in whom they have not
believed? And how shall they believe in Him of whom they
have not heard? And how shall they hear without a preacher?
And how shall they preach unless they are sent? As it is
written: "How beautiful are the feet of those who preach the
gospel of peace, who bring glad tidings of good things!". . . So
then faith comes by hearing, and hearing by the word of God.*

ROMANS 10:14–15, 17 NKJV

*Then the eyes of the blind shall be opened, and the ears of
the deaf shall be unstopped. Then the lame shall leap like a
deer, and the tongue of the dumb sing. For waters shall burst
forth in the wilderness, and streams in the desert.*

ISAIAH 35:5–6 NKJV

*A*bout the time the empire was preparing the
celebrations for Constantine's thirtieth year on the
throne, a revolt arose at some distance from Myra.

The imperial troops made an unexpected stop at
Nicholas's city, where their three commanders met the

archbishop. This proves that our dear Saint Nick, now an old man of eighty-five, was not only still alive but very active. He was an older senior citizen of the empire now, and yet he was about to do some of his most talked-about work. Saint Nicholas's life is a picture of the spiritual growth that should come with age.

❄

"Who is your superior?" Nicholas fired out upon being brought before the three commanders of the large army that was wreaking disaster upon Myra and its neighboring towns.

The three colonels looked at the man who stood before them like the wrath of God.

Virius Nepotianus humbly answered. "We are servants of our most excellent emperor, Constantine. We have been sent to quell a revolt that has broken out in a land some distance from here. Bad weather forced our ships upon your shores."

"Why then do you not follow your emperor in your conduct?"

The colonels were perplexed. "Sir, what do you mean?"

"When the emperor rode into battle he never allowed his men to seize whatever they wanted from cities he passed through. You are allowing that to happen."

The commanders were appalled to learn that this was happening. They personally disciplined their troops and order was quickly restored.

Nicholas was pleased. These three leaders were true soldiers of Constantine. Seeing a wrong, they used their power to right it. He prayed on their behalf. The three colonels gratefully accepted his prayers and felt special and somehow protected.

Nicholas had just finished when distraught members of his congregation arrived from Myra and fell at his feet, begging for his help.

"Tell me what has happened," he gently encouraged.

"In your absence Governor Eustathius has unjustly condemned to death Stavros, Pavlos, and Ioannis. They are to be executed today."

Nicholas knew these men personally. He knew they were innocent. "I must go to them!" Turning, he started running. After only a moment of stunned hesitation the three commanders quickly followed the older man who seemed to fly before them!

Along the way Nicholas met people who reported how the men were even now being dragged to the execution site. Nicholas ran faster.

When they came to the place, a multitude of people were crying. Nicholas saw that the executioner's sword was in the air ready to strike the first man. He rushed forward, grabbed the

*razor-sharp blade, threw it to the ground, and
set the men free.*

*Everyone gasped as Nicholas turned to
the executioner, whose arms were the size of
tree trunks. "You will not harm so much as a
hair on these innocent men's heads," Nicholas
commanded.*

*With utmost respect, the executioner bowed
before Nicholas, picked up his sword, and
turning, quietly left the site.*

*The three colonels looked at one another.
They had just witnessed a great miracle. Who
ever heard of an old man snatching a sword
from an executioner's grasp? Not even they,
seasoned soldiers, would attempt such a thing.
They would never forget what Nicholas did.
Nor would they forget the joy of the innocent
men who were now freed. They were leaping
around and singing in elation over their
miraculous deliverance. All the people joined
them!*

❆

It was an amazing event. But there's more to this
story. What happened to the governor, Eustathius—
the man who unjustly condemned the innocent ones?

Here, the story becomes one of repentance and
forgiveness, which is more important than the saving
of the innocent men's lives.

At first Eustathius tried to blame other innocent men. But Nicholas stood firm, and soon the governor expressed genuine repentance and a contrite heart.

And those colonels, well, they learned a great lesson about the God of Nicholas. In fact, a few short months later. . .

Well wait. . .

That story must be told later in this Advent calendar!

Prepare Your Heart for Christmas

The gift of forgiveness is probably the most important gift we can give during this time of year. Is there someone you know who is in need of the Lord's forgiveness? Let your feet be "beautiful" as you bring them the "gospel of peace" of "glad tidings of good things."

Please help me, Lord, to have "beautiful feet" that bring glad tidings of good things—knowledge about You to a world that so desperately needs your healing and saving love! Amen.

Dedication of Churches in Jerusalem

*Then the LORD said to Moses, "See, I have chosen
Bezalel son of Uri. . .and I have filled him with the
Spirit of God, with wisdom, with understanding,
with knowledge and with all kinds of skills—to make
artistic designs for work in gold, silver and bronze."*

EXODUS 31:1–4 NIV

*Jesus said to them, "Why are you bothering this woman?
She has done a beautiful thing to me. The poor you will
always have with you, but you will not always have me.
When she poured this perfume on my body, she did it to
prepare me for burial. Truly I tell you, wherever this gospel
is preached throughout the world, what she has done
will also be told, in memory of her."*

MATTHEW 26:10–13 NIV

*"Why do you seek the living among the dead?
He is not here, but is risen!"*

LUKE 24:5–6 NKJV

$\mathcal{I}$t is possible that Nicholas attended the Council of Tyre (it concerned the Arians, again) and then went to the dedication of the Basilica of Witness and the Church of the Resurrection (today nothing remains of the Basilica of Witness, but the rebuilt Church of the Resurrection is also called the Church of the Holy Sepulchre).

He'd visited the sites of the Crucifixion and the Resurrection when he was just a young priest on his first pilgrimage to the Holy Land. At that time, the sites had been covered up by pagan temples and statues.

In 325 Constantine asked his elderly mother, Helen—now his empress—to travel to the Holy Land and recover these sites before they were lost to history. Constantine wanted to honor the Lord and build houses of prayer for His people.

The dedication of these churches would have been a moving time for eighty-five-year-old Nicholas. But because the Arians were again causing trouble in the Church, he would have gone to the dedication of this beautiful church complex the same way he had years earlier—in disguise.

Or so he thought. . . .

The ceremony in Jerusalem had finished. The day was coming to a close. But it was one day

Nicholas didn't want to end.

He walked from the beautiful Basilica of Witness—which honored Christ's sacrifice on Calvary—the length of the open courtyard toward the site of Jesus' Resurrection. Tears filled Nicholas's eyes.

"I feel it, too." A man spoke by his side, startling Nicholas. Nicholas turned and saw that it was Eusebius, the historian and the emperor's close friend. Eusebius had delivered a beautiful speech during the dedication.

Nicholas smiled. "So much has changed in the world from when I first came here as a young man. Magnificently so!"

Eusebius looked out over the site and nodded. "But don't you mean from when you were just a young priest, Nicholas of Myra?"

Nicholas was surprised that the well-known bishop of Caesarea had recognized him.

"I remember you from the Nicene Council." Eusebius rubbed his check. "I wouldn't want to get on your wrong side."

Nicholas took a deep breath. "Today is a day for joy, not for controversy." His eyes darkened as he admitted, "But I wouldn't have been able to refrain myself from defending the nature of Christ had I come openly." Many followers of Arius had been present.

Eusebius nodded and silently agreed not to broach the subject. The wonders God had performed through Nicholas's faith encouraged him to agree with Nicholas. God loved this man. Eusebius believed everyone in the world—except perhaps the Arians—did.

Nicholas waved out over the complex. "This must please our Lord."

"We humans are so puny, but God does appreciate our efforts. Constantine is a wise man. One I admire greatly."

Nicholas nodded. "What a man in a position of responsibility can do. . . He has taken what God has given him and changed the world more than any man except"—Nicholas glanced back at the marble basilica that gleamed in the late evening sunlight like a jewel—"the God-Man who gave His life for the world right there."

Eusebius turned in the other direction toward the Anastasis (Resurrection) with its beautiful dome that was still under construction. "And rose again there!"

"Alleluia!" Nicholas sang out.

"Alleluia!" Eusebius echoed.

❄

To see such an event honoring the life of Christ!

Church buildings aren't necessary to worship the Lord. But except to care for each other, animals, and the earth is there any better way to spend our hard-earned money than to honor Jesus by using our resources to build houses of prayer?

The Lord was pleased with the women when they poured out the costly oil on His head and feet (see above and John 12:3). To have been those women! But they were the only two women that we know of who were blessed to do this act of worship. But in building beautiful structures—that is something everyone can have a part in.

What a beautiful way to tell the Lord that we love Him.

And there's no better time than when we go to our houses of prayer during Advent!

Prepare Your Heart for Christmas

Advent is a good time of the year to rethink our spending priorities and personal consumption. For instance, is it better to live in modest homes and give some of our money to a church that honors God? This goes for food and clothing and other things, too. Should we keep buying more and more for ourselves, or should we, seeing a need, help others instead?

Please help me, Lord, never to forget the sacrifice You—the King of the universe—made for me. Amen.

THE GOD OF NICHOLAS

Which things are an allegory.
GALATIANS 4:24 KJV

*For thus says the LORD: After seventy years are completed
at Babylon, I will visit you and perform My good word
toward you, and cause you to return to this place. . . .
Then you will call upon Me and go and pray to Me,
and I will listen to you. . . . I will be found by you, says
the LORD, and I will bring you back from your captivity.*
JEREMIAH 29:10, 12, 14 NKJV

A couple of months later Nicholas again meets
up with the three commanders.

Although a true story, it is also allegorical. It's set
during our age—the Age of Grace—when the Lord
said, " 'If you have faith and do not doubt. . .whatever
things you ask in prayer, believing, you will receive' "
(Matthew 21:21–22 NKJV). It shows that we live in a
more gracious time than any other. Today we are truly
a "blessed generation."

The three colonels returned victoriously to New Rome, and Constantine was extremely pleased with them for having put down the revolt. He promoted them to the rank of general and made them a part of his close circle of advisers.

But certain other advisers were envious of the generals. Evil was in their hearts. They approached the emperor's chief steward, Avlavios, with lies and bribes and nearly changed the course of history.

Let's see!

"It is true, Avlavios. The emperor thinks the generals are his friends, but they actually have treason in their hearts," said one of Constantine's advisers.

"In what way?" asked Avlavios.

"The emperor thinks they put down the revolt last summer. But they actually made a secret agreement with the rebels. When the time is right they will revolt against Constantine," the second adviser said.

"I can't believe it! Everyone knows that treason is the one thing Constantine cannot abide."

The advisers looked at one another. They were counting on it. "We assure you, it's true." These advisers were envious of the three generals' close position to the emperor. "We are prepared to back up our word with our personal wealth and assurance for your continued good graces."

Avlavios understood. There would not only be extra earnings for him if he acted on this report but also, if it was true—and he had no reason to doubt the sincerity of these advisers—he was being assured that his position would stay secure. "Very well, I will have the generals detained until we get to the bottom of this. There is no need to trouble the emperor with these events until then."

"But why?" Nepotianus shouted out as he and his shocked comrades were shoved inside the dungeon. "I demand to know what the charge against us is!"

Their jailers laughed and dangled heavy pouches in front of them. "Who cares? We've got our gold!"

"We are innocent!" Ursus shouted while he supported his friend Herpylion who had nearly fainted at the turn of events.

"You think that makes a difference to us?" The biggest of the bribed guards snickered. "You wouldn't let us take from Myra last summer"—he threw the heavy pouch up in the air and caught it victoriously—"we only got what loot was coming to us."

"You are no soldier of Constantine," Nepotianus declared.

"Maybe not. But neither are you any longer. You are criminals." He snickered again and slammed the door in the faces of the men who had been his superiors but were now his prisoners.

In the near darkness the generals huddled together. For days that turned to weeks, they waited for salvation. But the world was dark. They were almost certain that they had been forgotten by God and men.

✳

Three hundred years earlier, just before the birth of Christ, the Jews thought that the Lord had forgotten them, too.

And when they were finally remembered, to have been forgotten almost seemed the better choice to many of them. Help didn't come as they were expecting it—with blazing lights of truth, justice, freedom, and spectacular supernatural power. Help came in the form of a little baby and later, a cross.

With the threat of the executioner's sword hanging over their heads, the three generals finally remembered another execution that had been prevented by the brave archbishop of Myra.

The Secretary of State Symeon the Metaphrastes wrote that the three generals prayed their hearts out to God all night long: "O Lord God of our holy father, Nicholas, who delivered three men at Myra from an unjust death, overcome, O Lord, this evil which threatens us and overlook not this injustice. . . . Rescue us from the hands of our enemies. Come unto our aid, lest we should die tomorrow."

Their "tomorrow" might have been only a few hours away, but it was more than enough time for God to bring the generals "back from captivity" and commend His servant Nicholas to the world.

Prepare Your Heart for Christmas

This is the "Season of Light," but since we live in a world seeped in sin, dark moments can still come to our souls. In your darkest moments, do you turn to the Lord Jesus Christ for help? He came as a little baby so we always could. It's up to us to do so now more than ever.

Heavenly Father, help me to always turn to You for help in my darkest moments—just like the three generals. Amen.

HOTLINE FROM GOD!

*Now in the second year of Nebuchadnezzar's reign,
Nebuchadnezzar had dreams; and his spirit
was so troubled that his sleep left him.*

DANIEL 2:1 NKJV

*"Very truly I tell you, whoever believes in me will do the
works I have been doing, and they will do even greater
things than these, because I am going to the Father."*

JOHN 14:12 NIV

*Now when they came up out of the water, the Spirit of the
Lord caught Philip away, so that the eunuch saw him no
more; and he went on his way rejoicing. But Philip was
found at Azotus. And passing through, he preached
in all the cities till he came to Caesarea.*

ACTS 8:39–40 NKJV

The prayer of the three generals is similar to what
the Jews prayed to God so many times before the
coming of Christ.

Did God answer those generals' prayers?

God answers all prayers. But sometimes we like His answers more than at other times. The crossing of the Red Sea, Daniel in the lion's den, and Deacon Philip and the Ethiopian all come to mind. This was also one of those times.

Because of bad advisers God's emperor, Constantine, was about to make a grave mistake. He was about to condemn innocent men.

What did the generals do? They prayed to God. God not only freed the generals, but He sent Nicholas to "visit" Constantine in a dream, and commended Nicholas to all.

This is one of the many reasons people today still remember Saint Nick! God wanted us to remember him and his great faith, a faith all believers can learn from as these generals did—until their own faith grows to maturity.

Constantine awoke with a start. At least, he thought he was awake. But he wasn't sure. Maybe he was dreaming that he was awake. It wouldn't be the first time. His soldier's instincts, however, told him that he wasn't alone.

"Who's there?"

"Rise quickly, O Emperor," the figure replied. Constantine was already on his feet, sword in hand. The emperor couldn't see the man too

clearly in the predawn hours, but the man's next words astounded him.

"Release the three generals. They are innocent. You have been given false information concerning them!"

"Are you referring to Nepotianus, Ursus, and Herpylion?" Constantine had had a hard time falling asleep that night. He had these men on his mind. Of all his generals he had thought he could trust them the most. Their treachery cut deep.

"They are innocent!" the man affirmed angrily. "If you do not free them, you will perish."

"Who are you?" Constantine asked. The man seemed somehow familiar to him, and yet, in the fogginess of the moment, he couldn't place him.

"I am Nicholas of Myra. God has sent me forth to stop you from doing a great wrong."

At hearing the name Constantine was suddenly awake but also confused. "Nicholas of Myra. . . ?" The man was no longer there. Without pause, Constantine bellowed out for Avlavios to come to him. Something was very wrong. This was either pagan priests using sorcery and magic—two things Constantine particularly hated because he knew they went against God—or else he was about to have three innocent men executed. He shivered. Whatever *it was, he needed to get to the bottom of it. Now.*

Avlavios was more than shaken in his own chambers. The bishop of Myra had "visited" him, too.

"Why did you accept money and harm those three men who committed no offence?" the bishop demanded.

"I. . ." Avlavios hadn't known how to respond. "The other advisers said that insurgents would soon break the three generals out of prison and set up a revolt against Constantine. I had no reason to doubt them."

"You know that it's not true! You will set this right or else your life will be taken from you!"

At that moment Avlavios wished nothing more than to set things right. When a messenger came from the palace for him to appear before the emperor, Avlavios made haste.

❋

As the Bible tells us, God can do whatever He wants to do. That night He wanted to correct a great evil that was about to take place and to commend His friend Nicholas to the emperor, the generals, and all the world. He wanted to use one great Christian to get through to another!

Today, Nicholas would probably just pick up the phone, put a call through to the emperor, and tell him something bad was brewing in his administration. Back in the fourth century though, dreams and visions were the fastest mode of communication—people listened to them. They were "hotlines."

Nicholas explained everything in detail to Constantine and then told him what would happen if he didn't stop the situation from escalating out of control: Constantine would perish by an evil death.

Not wanting to leave the emperor's chief adviser out of the loop, Nicholas was also sent by God to Avlavios.

Jesus gave us all a "hotline" to God after Pentecost. We just have to do like Constantine is about to do and take action.

Prepare Your Heart for Christmas

Has our technological world hindered our ability to "see and hear" the miraculous things of God? This Advent season choose one day where you voluntarily turn off all computers, TVs, phones, and radios in your home. See how acute your spiritual "hearing" becomes without these technological interferences.

Note: Technology is good (I personally like computers, TVs, and phones!). But quiet is better, and it should have a bigger place in our lives than we often give it (Psalm 46:10).

God, please help me to always see the miraculous moments sent by You. Don't let me be blinded by technology and science. First and foremost help me experience in full the blessed time of grace Your First Advent brought to our world. Amen.

No Magic Allowed!

*If a prophet, or one who foretells by dreams, appears
among you and. . .says, "Let us follow other gods" (gods
you have not known) "and let us worship them," you
must not listen to the words of that prophet.*

DEUTERONOMY 13:1–3 NIV

*Now for some time a man named Simon had practiced sorcery
in the city and amazed all the people of Samaria. He boasted
that he was someone great, and all the people, both high and
low, gave him their attention and exclaimed, "This man is
rightly called the Great Power of God." They followed him
because he had amazed them for a long time with his sorcery.*

ACTS 8:9–11 NIV

*"At that time if anyone says to you, 'Look, here is the
Messiah!' or, 'There he is!' do not believe it. For false
messiahs and false prophets will appear and perform
great signs and wonders to deceive, if possible, even
the elect. See, I have told you ahead of time."*

MATTHEW 24:23–25 NIV

$\mathcal{A}$s a student of scriptures, Constantine knew to be wary of dreams, signs, wonders, and people who proclaimed them. Before he could address the reason for the unusual visit to his chambers, he had to be sure that it was from God.

The deceptions and heresies of the Samaritan magician, Simon Magus (Acts 8:4–24), who "worked" during the time of Christ (Matthew 24:23–25) were remembered well. Just a few years earlier Constantine had enacted laws against magicians and sorcerers who used their magic arts against the minds of men.

Constantine had to ascertain what exactly had happened during the early hours of the morning before he could decide what to do.

And the three generals? Well, they were finally about to defend themselves before the emperor they loved and respected!

❋

"By what sorcery did you bring these dreams on us," Constantine demanded of the generals. Constantine had been shaken when he learned that Avlavios had also been visited in his chambers.

The three generals looked at one another. They had no idea what their emperor was talking about.

Constantine could see that they were

perplexed. Getting control of his own alarm, he spoke calmly and gently to the men. "Fear not. Speak to me as your friend."

Ursus said, "We know nothing of sorcery, nor have we ever spoken against you."

"God is our witness in this," Herpylion whispered.

"If it be otherwise, then we give our lives," Ursus said.

"And that of all our relatives, too," Nepotianus agreed.

Constantine sat back. He was certain now that these men had been wrongly accused. "Please give me an account of the whole story."

"Last summer," Nepotianus said, "while on our campaign to put down the revolt, bad weather forced us into the vicinity of Myra. . . ."

"Myra?" Constantine interjected. That was where the man in his vision said he was from. "Go on."

Nepotianus told about the innocent men the bishop there had saved and about the previous night when the three generals had found out that they were sentenced to die. "Desperate, we prayed to God with tears, asking that He help us and deliver us, remembering His great friend Nicholas of Myra. . . ."

"Nicholas of Myra. . ." Constantine repeated. With the speed of a lightning strike he knew where he had heard the name. He looked

over at Avlavios. "This is the man who struck Arius at the Great Council!"

Avlavios's lips trembled. "I believe so, sire."

Constantine marveled at the bishop from Myra's boldness. But of course it was him! Smiling, he turned to the three generals. "I'm sorry to say that it is not I who grants you your lives, but the servant of the Lord, Nicholas. Go to him and tell him that I fulfilled the command he gave me this morning. It's important that you deliver this message." He smiled again and said, "I do not want such a great servant of God as Nicholas of Myra angry with me!"

❋

No, Constantine definitely did not want Nicholas angry with him!

But by saying this, Constantine showed that although he was emperor, he knew that he was accountable to God and to God's servants. Especially servants as great as Nicholas of Myra!

But what about Avlavios, Constantine's chief of staff? After all, he took a bribe and was about to have innocent men executed. Isn't he like Haman in the book of Esther?

Without the Holy Spirit, now given to all who ask, Avlavios would have probably met the same end as Haman. But like Governor Eustathius of Myra,

Avlavios genuinely asked for pardon and it was given to him (unlike Simon Magus in Acts 8:22–24).

Advent is a wonderful time of year to forgive, in the name of Christ, those who have wronged us. To pardon and then celebrate the birth of the Savior. Isn't that one of the things that Christmas is all about?

But remember. . .no sorcery or magic (which is an attempt to control creation for a person's own advantage) is allowed.

Because God's ways are so much greater!

Prepare Your Heart for Christmas

Often people refer to "Christmas magic." But does "magic" have any part in Christmas or Christ's ministry? (Hint: Definitely not!)

> *Dear Lord in heaven, help me not to be fooled*
> *by false prophets, signs, and wonders but to test*
> *everything as Constantine tested his early-*
> *morning visit from Saint Nick. Amen.*

A Beautiful Finale!

Make a joyful noise unto the LORD, all ye lands.
PSALM 100:1 KJV

*And the ransomed of the LORD shall return, and
come to Zion with singing, with everlasting joy on
their heads. They shall obtain joy and gladness,
and sorrow and sighing shall flee away.*
ISAIAH 35:10 NKJV

*And suddenly there was with the angel a
multitude of the heavenly host praising God.*
LUKE 2:13 NKJV

*I*t was a happy day in Myra when the generals
returned to town!

That is. . .once the people understood their
reason for coming.

At first they were probably uneasy at seeing the
generals' mighty warship sail into their harbor.

But once their archbishop heard who had arrived,

he soon put the people's minds at ease. He knew then that his "visit" to the emperor had been successful. Saint Nick's old heart rejoiced. The man he'd been praying for all his life—the first Christian emperor—had stayed the course. The government would continue to legally allow the spread of the Gospel.

This moment was a high point in Nicholas's life. It would have been like the president of the United States awarding him the Medal of Honor (or the Presidential Medal of Freedom).

*

Nicholas stood on the portico of the church surrounded by the children from the orphanage. They waited as the festive military parade made its way up the main roadway of Myra toward them.

Shouts of joy and celebration filled the air. The people of Myra were happy. That made the old archbishop's eyes twinkle in the way the people of Myra loved. They all knew how his eyes could flash with righteous anger, too, and no one wanted to be on the receiving end of that!

This day though, that special look was for the mighty military generals who bowed low before Nicholas. "Our good emperor has sent us to you with a message." The oldest general spoke so all could hear. "He said, 'I fulfilled your command. Please, servant of Christ, do not be angry with me.'"

Nicholas closed his eyes in thanksgiving. "I'm not angry with our fine emperor. I am thankful that God put such a Christian man on the throne during my lifetime."

The generals smiled. Turning, Nepotianus took something from his lieutenant.

A sound of awe went up from the people as he gave a Gospel bound in gold to Nicholas and Ursus presented an incense burner made of gleaming gold and precious stones. When Herpylion gave Nicholas two exquisite gold lamps, the people stood quietly in wonder of it all. The workmanship of the items—made with love to God's glory—was evident to all.

"These our emperor awards to your church, great servant of the Lord, in the name of the Lord Jesus Christ."

Nicholas handed the precious items to the children so they could touch and see them up close. "In our precious Lord's name, I accept them with much thanksgiving."

Nepotianus looked at the children. "We"— he motioned to the other two generals—"also want to show our gratitude to you for being such a great servant of the Lord and helping us." He motioned for three large chests to be placed before the archbishop. "Please use this gold in any way you see fit."

Between his mustache and his beard,
Nicholas's smile became even wider. Using the
gold of God's earth to make others' lives happier
and safer—particularly the lives of children—
was his specialty!

✳

These awards from Constantine to Nicholas were
unlike the Medal of Honor in one important way:
These military leaders were presenting this award
from their commander-in-chief to the church in Myra
in the name of Christ.

God was the One being honored by this award, not
Nicholas, not the emperor, and not the government.

Nicholas, the three generals, the people, and
even Constantine understood that it was God's power
that had kept their commander-in-chief from a great
wrong, one that could have greatly hindered the
spread of the Lord's Gospel throughout history.

Constantine once again gave honor to the little
baby—Jesus—who came into the world at Christmas
and gave His holy life for it at Easter.

The three generals, Nicholas, Constantine, and
the people were remembering and honoring God,
whereas the envious advisers were soundly defeated by
God's work (See December 18).

A beautiful finale to the *Account of the Three
Generals*—and all because of the Lord's First Advent!

Prepare Your Heart for Christmas

Often to have a really perfect Christmas we have
to plan and work for it in advance. But oh. . .the
joy when friends and family get together and
share a loving and fun time of singing and praying
and feasting on December the 25th! And when
unexpected things happen—like a surprise visit from
someone who lives far away—how much better
the moment becomes! Keep your eyes open for the
unexpected this year!

*Dear Lord in heaven, thank You for those moments of
joy that come unexpectedly into our daily lives, just as it
came to the shepherds the night Christ was born and to
the people of Myra the day the generals returned to town.
Amen.*

DEDICATION OF THE CHURCH OF THE NATIVITY

"Therefore the Lord Himself will give you a sign: Behold, the virgin shall conceive and bear a Son, and shall call His name Immanuel."
ISAIAH 7:14 NKJV

But when the fulness of the time was come, God sent forth his Son, made of a woman, made under the law.
GALATIANS 4:4 KJV

For unto you is born this day in the city of David a Saviour, which is Christ the Lord. And this shall be a sign unto you; ye shall find the babe wrapped in swaddling clothes, lying in a manger.
LUKE 2:11–12 KJV

*N*icholas returned to his home away from home—Beit Jala!

The dedication of the Church of the Nativity, commissioned by Constantine thirteen years earlier, was about to take place.

Because of how greatly Nicholas had always defended the two natures of Christ (His divine and human) against heresies, this place where God took on humanity was probably even more special to him than the dedication he'd attended six years earlier in Jerusalem (See December 17).

When he had lived close to Bethlehem after his imprisonment, the site of the Lord's birth had been marred by a temple built to a pagan god. But thanks to Constantine (and his mother, Helen), no longer!

❄

Nicholas stood in the early morning and gazed down into the cave below him. His eyes were trained on the actual spot where the Lord of Glory had been born of the Virgin Mary. Nicholas was glad for the balustrade's support. He felt weak in his knees as emotions nearly overwhelmed his almost ninety-year-old body.

He looked from the manger to the building that was being dedicated. It was a magnificent basilica with an octagonal focus, where Nicholas and his companion, Timothy, the son of the current innkeeper in Bethlehem, now stood. There was a hole in the center of the roof directly above the silver manger. It let the sunlight shine on the birthplace of the Light of the world.

"How they found the holy cave still amazes me," Nicholas said to his young companion.

"My father was told by his father where it was, and his father was told by his, and his father by his. . .so it was all the way back," Timothy explained.

"So when the Empress Helen came on behalf of her son, Constantine, looking for the site. . ."

"We knew where it was!"

"The spoken word," Nicholas said, "it's mighty."

"My ancestors knew that its location shouldn't be forgotten, especially after the Lord's death and Resurrection." He paused. "The Emperor Hadrian tried to cover up the sites of the Lord's life so many times. But he couldn't do it."

"It really doesn't matter to Jesus' work whether we have these locations or any church buildings. . . ."

Timothy gave a quick laugh. "But after so many years of not being allowed to have them, it's an honor to worship Him in places built just for Him. . ."

"I couldn't agree more. My parents, my uncle, and your grandfather would have loved this." Nicholas spoke wistfully. "But until Constantine, persecutions prevented them from building such places of worship."

Timothy nodded and pointed toward the basilica to the west. It extended for about eighty

feet, and two rows of columns on either side of
the nave created four side aisles. Four porticoes
enclosed a square, open courtyard at the other
end. "It's so beautiful."

"But even if this memorial doesn't last,
Timothy, as long as the earth remains, this spot
is marked for all generations to remember where
the God of Glory came to earth, fully human
and fully divine!"

* * *

Although the first Church of the Nativity was
destroyed in approximately 530, the Emperor
Justinian I rebuilt the church during subsequent
years, and much of what pilgrims see today is from
that reconstruction. But there is a mosaic from the
late fourth century in Rome that shows the original
Church of the Nativity in Bethlehem. It was a
beautiful memorial to Christ indeed!

This brings to mind that without the birth of
Christ we wouldn't have something we take for
granted—our beloved church buildings. Those
structures—of so many shapes and styles—that
grace so many of our towns (and our Christmas
cards!) are such an important part of our lives.

But to have been at the dedication of the original
church built in honor of Christ's birth at the spot
where it occurred. . .what a moving event in the life
of Saint Nick!

Prepare Your Heart for Christmas

Consider during this Advent season how important your church building is to you. How would you feel if you were told you couldn't have it?

Dear Lord, thank You for being born a little baby in a shepherd's cave in order to save. . .me. Amen.

Jesus—
The Way to the Tree of Life

*Then the LORD God said, "Behold, the man has become like
one of Us, to know good and evil. And now, lest he put out
his hand and take also of the tree of life, and eat, and live
forever"—therefore the LORD God sent him out of the garden
of Eden. . . He drove out the man; and He placed cherubim
at the east of the garden of Eden, and a flaming sword which
turned every way, to guard the way to the tree of life.*

Genesis 3:22–24 NKJV

*Blessed are those who do His commandments, that they may
have the right to the tree of life, and may enter through the
gates into the city. But outside are dogs and sorcerers and
sexually immoral and murderers and idolaters, and whoever
loves and practices a lie. "I, Jesus, have sent My angel to testify
to you these things in the churches. I am the Root and the
Offspring of David, the Bright and Morning Star.". . .
He who testifies to these things says, "Surely I am coming
quickly." Amen. Even so, come, Lord Jesus!*

Revelation 22:14–16, 20 NKJV

*S*aint Nicholas was a sailor from a very young age.
So coming to the aid of sailors caught on the sea in hurricane-force winds and steering their ship safely through it was something he knew how to do. It was easy for him. Getting him to the ship however, well, that was easy for God to do. After all, Jesus had walked on water (Matthew 14:25–31) and then told His disciples that they would do even greater things than He (John 14:12) because He was going to the Father. All they needed was faith. Faith was something Nicholas had in abundance.

The miracle isn't that Nicholas, in answer to the sailors' prayers, was miraculously sent by God to guide them to a safe harbor. It was nice that he was God's instrument to save them from bodily harm— we all welcome such Godly intervention—but the real miracle, the one that had eternal consequences, is what came afterward. That Nicholas, being the great servant of God, "steered" those sailors to the Tree of Life, the very reason for Christmas after all!

Let's see!

*The sailors fell at Nicholas's feet in thanksgiving.
Although none of them had ever seen him in
person, they knew he was the one who had
saved them from certain death on the churning*

Mediterranean Sea. "Thank you, great servant of God! If it hadn't been for you we would have drowned." The captain spoke for them all.

"My children." Nicholas went from each man and raised them to their feet.

But they would not be quieted. They wanted the entire city to know of their miraculous deliverance from drowning.

After letting them speak to the multitude who had gathered, Nicholas said something these hardened sailors weren't expecting. "Now dear children, consider carefully the hidden things of your hearts. Even if people do not see—God does." The sailors looked at him in guilty and concerned disbelief. Nicholas raised his brows, challenging each of them to confront their sins. "Paul has said, 'Don't you know that you yourselves are God's temple and that God's Spirit dwells in your midst?'" (1 Corinthians 3:16 NIV).

After coming close to dying, their hearts were opened to God. They knew what Nicholas was saying. They each had a woman in every port, and this sin was on their hearts.

"You do not want to be alienated from God," Nicholas continued. "We were sent out of the Garden. But with the Birth of the Lord Jesus Christ and His saving work on the cross, we have been given the way back to the Tree of Life."

They looked at him in question, just as they had on the ship. He answered their silent plea. "It's through the precious blood and body of our Lord Jesus Christ. The very One who saved your bodies from drowning in the sea now wishes to save your souls from 'drowning.'"

"Dear Father." The sailors again fell at Nicholas's feet, confessed their sins, and before they went on their way once again, they were new men in Christ!

They left Myra and set sail again. They not only told all they met around the world about the Lord Jesus Christ but about His servant Nicholas and how he had saved them from drowning in the sea. . .and on dry land.

Saint Nicholas had showed them the way to the Tree of Life!

＊

Jesus' ministry of healing shows how often the needs of the body were taken care of before the needs of the soul and spirit of man.

Nicholas spent his entire life of service imitating the Lord. It is another reason why he is often known as a gift giver.

He didn't neglect any part of the human: the body, the soul, or the spirit. And he always met people where they were: in sailing ships, in dreams, on the executioner's field, in churches, on a city street, or even in their homes. All human needs—physical, mental, and spiritual—were his concern. As God's servant, he went wherever the Lord Jesus sent him.

Prepare Your Heart for Christmas

Consider on this eve of Christmas Eve, do we go where God sends us? Or do we make excuses for not following His will for our lives?

Jesus, please send me where You want me to go and give me the faith to follow Your will. Amen.

Christmas Eve
Jolly Old Saint Nicholas
and Children

*"The glory of the LORD shall be revealed, and all flesh shall see
it together; for the mouth of the LORD has spoken."*
ISAIAH 40:5 NKJV

*Love the LORD your God with all your heart and with all your
soul and with all your strength. These commandments. . .
Impress them on your children. Talk about them when you
sit at home and when you walk along the road, when you
lie down and when you get up. Tie them as symbols on your
hands and bind them on your foreheads.*
DEUTERONOMY 6:5–8 NIV

*Jesus said, "Let the little children come to me,
and do not hinder them, for the kingdom of heaven
belongs to such as these." When he had placed his
hands on them, he went on from there.*
MATTHEW 19:14–15 NIV

*F*or the first time in his long life, Nicholas was feeling poorly.

He knew that his old body had run its course and that very soon he would be meeting his Maker face-to-face.

Far from distressing Nicholas, it made him happy. He was ready to go to his eternal home, ready to be greeted by his parents and uncle; his childhood friend Pericles; Pericles's son Petros; the Emperor Constantine and his mother, Helen; his first helpers in Myra, Paul and Theodore; and all the other people he had met during his life as well as all the Christians—the apostles even—who had lived before him.

But leaving the children of his congregation— and at the age of ninety-five that meant practically everyone!—that was hard for him. Especially as the days came closer to the Nativity of the Lord, and he knew that his time on earth was coming to a close.

This part of Nicholas's life isn't sad, but it is one of real human emotion on the part of Nicholas and those who loved him.

❋

"Are the children here?" Nicholas asked his faithful friend, Yorgos, as the much younger priest helped him walk toward the garden.

"They have prepared a special 'throne' in the center of them all just for you," Yorgos said

as they passed slowly through the door. "They have another surprise, too!"

Nicholas's eyes twinkled as he held out his hand to the Mediterranean sun that shone strong and warm this November day. "I'm so blessed. . ."

The sound of voices raised in song stopped Nicholas. "The children are singing my favorite hymn!"

They turned the corner, and when the children saw their beloved archbishop, they all beamed at him while some of the younger children waved. Nicholas waved back and stood smiling at the multitude of children and their parents in the garden and those beyond in the street. The words of the hymn from the second chapter of Philippians washed over him, but when they got to the part "that at the name of Jesus every knee should bow, in heaven and on earth and under the earth," Nicholas did what he had always done at hearing these words. Leaning on Yorgos, he knelt his ninety-five-year-old body down to the ground.

The people looked at one another in amazement! He had been so ill the last week, and yet, still, he knelt before the Lord! With thanksgiving everyone in the garden did, too. No one arose until the final words of the hymn: "And every tongue acknowledge that Jesus Christ is Lord, to the glory of God the Father!"

"Amen!" Nicholas's voice, stronger than it had been in a while, sang out.

"Amen!" All the people sang back then surged forward to greet him. He put his hand on everyone as he shuffled slowly through the crowd toward the "throne" they had prepared for him.

"Aah," he said as he sat. "These old bones say a mighty big thank-you for this comfortable seat." Everyone's smiles widened even more. "Now, I want each one of you to come forward and whisper in my ear your most important prayer. I will pray to the Lord that it might be so."

The happy sounds of children and their parents filled the air. They all knew that the Lord listened carefully to the prayers of this man of extreme faith! One by one they came forward. The smallest even got to sit on his lap!

Later that day, none could be sure who enjoyed themselves more, the multitude of children Nicholas greeted and listened to or the dear archbishop himself!

Nicholas would have said he did, of course!

❄

Saint Nick loved children, and children loved him! He did everything in his power to protect them from evil people and evil times. But he knew that the best way to do that was by giving them knowledge of the Lord Jesus Christ. That was the greatest gift one human could give to another.

Saint Peter said to the lame man in Acts 3 (NIV): "Silver or gold I do not have, but what I do have I give you. In the name of Jesus Christ of Nazareth, walk." He set the standard with those words as to what all Christians should give to one another: the gift of passing on the greatest information ever given to the world—the name, knowledge, and saving grace of the Lord Jesus Christ!

Older generations, and parents especially, must tell young children, fresh from God's creative hand, about Jesus. Moses gave this commandment before crossing the Jordan, and Jesus repeated it during His ministry.

Saint Nicholas proved faithful to this command all his earthly life, and his way of treating children with respect and love was an example that has carried all the way to our times.

Children loved Saint Nicholas.

They still do!

Prepare Your Heart for Christmas

On this Christmas Eve, gather your friends and family all together, go to church, and hear the Christmas story. It can never be heard or told too often.

Father, let me always treat Your little children with respect, recognizing that it's only their bodies that are small, not their hearts and not their souls! Most often little children understand the things of God better than me! Amen.

Merry Christmas!
Saint Nicholas. . ."Santa Claus"

*In the beginning was the Word, and the Word
was with God, and the Word was God.*
John 1:1 kjv

*"The virgin will conceive and give birth to a son, and they
will call him Immanuel" (which means "God with us").*
Matthew 1:23 niv

*N*ot everyone is blessed to be born into a
Christian family. Many people who come from
lands and families that aren't traditionally Christian
would never have had the chance to learn about Jesus
without the controversial modern "myth" of "Santa
Claus."

In his North American alter ego, Nicholas of
Myra is brought into the lives of people who would
not otherwise celebrate Christ's Nativity. Often,
non-Christians don't know what they are actually

celebrating at Christmastime. But through Santa Claus, Nicholas is still witnessing the Lord Jesus Christ. With just a little searching, people who might not have heard about the birth of Christ do!

So maybe the watered-down, commercially overused "Santa Claus" isn't as bad as some might think. . .especially when we learn about the life of the real Saint Nicholas. The important thing to remember is that the real Saint Nick loved Jesus all the days of his long life.

That's something to trust and imitate!

*

Gasps of joy came from around the church building when their archbishop walked in supported by the young priest Yorgos.

Two days after visiting with the children, Nicholas's health had taken a turn for the worse. Everyone had been sad that he wouldn't be here today to speak the words he always spoke this first day of Advent. But now they would be blessed to once again hear his voice proclaim the Word to them.

As he walked forward with the aid of Yorgos, they could see that he was frail. He seemed to be fading away before their eyes. His long beard was thin and as white as snow, his once strong olive complexion was so pale that his veins stood out beneath his taut skin, his slender back was bent.

But when he turned and faced them, his eyes—oh, how they twinkled! And his lips were turned upward in a joyful smile while his soul seemed to enfold them all. Although his body was tired, Nicholas was radiant.

Everyone sat in quiet expectation.

"'In the beginning,'" their dear archbishop said, "'was the Word, and the Word was with God, and the Word was God.'" Everyone smiled as the familiar and much-loved words washed over them, and his beautiful voice once again proclaimed Jesus. His voice wasn't as strong as it used to be, even a month earlier, but that didn't matter. It rang clear and with truth. "'He was with God in the beginning.'" Nicholas paused and gazed out over them all. "'Through him all things were made. Without him nothing was made that has been made. In him was life.'" His voice rose. "'And that life was the light of all mankind,'" he went on slowly, and when he came to the last line, he looked upward and with his eyes closed sang the words to the Lord. "'The Word became flesh. . .and made his dwelling among us.'" When the last note settled, there wasn't a dry eye in the room. Everyone waited.

He opened his eyes and looked out over them all. His breathing was labored, but still he spoke. "My beloved children." He paused. "I had hoped to be with you. . .for one more Nativity of the Lord." His voice cracked. He *couldn't go on. He was ready to go to the Lord but in a very human way sad to leave these, his children.*

Yorgos, who hadn't left his side, smiled at him and spoke for the entire congregation when he said, "Dear Nicholas of Myra, somehow I think you will be with us all for every Nativity of the Lord always!"

❄

He has been!

More than any other person—other than the Lord and His mother—it has been Nicholas of Myra who is most remembered during this time of year.

Even though the commercial world might try, "Santa Claus" can't be totally separated from Saint Nicholas. His life and faith shine through as a beacon and a starting point to search for the God whom Nicholas loved and served all his life. He has been God's ambassador throughout the centuries.

Nicholas of Myra, Saint Nicholas, Saint Nick. . . Santa Claus. . . *

The man of great faith who loved Jesus!

Prepare Your Heart for Christmas

Consider how important celebrating Advent and Christmas really is to the world.

Dear Lord in heaven, thank You for this glorious time of year when we remember Your birth. Please help us always to be faithful to You as Nicholas of Myra was his whole life. Come, Lord Jesus, come! Amen.

*Note: In Greek Nicholas's name is "Nikolaos," and it means "victory of the people." In Dutch—how he "arrived" in America—it is "San Nicolaas." Americans said it fast with a stress on the broad double *a* of the last syllable, and a *t* slipped in, giving us "Santy Claus," just a short stop on the way to "Santa Claus." But it all means the same thing—our beloved Saint Nicholas!

Conclusion

"His master replied, 'Well done, good and faithful servant! You have been faithful with a few things; I will put you in charge of many things. Come and share your master's happiness!'"

MATTHEW 25:21 NIV

can't tell you what an honor it has been for me to be with you during these glorious days leading up to the birth of Christ. The faith of that dear Christian, Nicholas of Myra, has challenged me to rise to new heights in my faith. There is always something new to learn when studying his outstanding life—I should know as I've been doing it for nearly two decades!—and in these pages, the growing of my faith has been my reward.

If Nicholas of Myra can do all he did during the dynamic time in history he lived in, through his total trust in Jesus Christ, then isn't that what we should be doing, too? His witness and his legacy is mighty! Saint Nicholas has been a part of our Christmas traditions for the last 1700 years because of his life, faith, and leadership.

I hope your Christmas celebration is filled with family, friends, food, shared memories of past Christmases, but mostly, during the busyness of the day, I hope you have quiet moments, too. Because it is when all is calm and still that our faith has the time to grow as we read the Nativity story, worship the Lord in the sacredness of the day, and deeply experience the culmination of this Advent season. That is the true "Christmas feeling!"

Merry Christmas from Saint Nicholas. . .and me!

Ann Nichols
www.stnicholasandchristmas.com